ART AND MUSIC
TOOLKIT

Dedication
To the Whitefield Institute and Oliver Barclay for their support and encouragement without which this book would not have been written.

ART AND MUSIC

TOOLKIT

Margaret Cooling
with
Colin Humphreys and Philip King

BRITISH AND FOREIGN BIBLE SOCIETY
Stonehill Green, Westlea, SWINDON SN5 7DG

© Margaret Cooling 1996
Music section © Colin Humphreys and Philip King 1996

First published 1996

All rights reserved. No part of this publication may be reproduced, stored in a retrieval system, or transmitted, in any form or by any means, electronic, mechanical, photocopying (except as specified on page 4), recording or otherwise without the prior permission of The British and Foreign Bible Society. The right of Margaret Cooling, Colin Humphreys and Philip King to be identified as the authors of this work has been asserted by them in accordance with the Copyright, Designs and Patents Act 1988.

Unless otherwise stated, quotations from the Bible are from the Good News Bible, published by the Bible Societies/HarperCollins Publications Ltd UK © American Bible Society, New York 1966, 1971, 1976 and 1992.

A catalogue record for this book is available from the British Library ISBN 0564 088552

Printed in Great Britain by Ebenezer Baylis Ltd.

Cover design by Jane Taylor

Music section by Colin Humphreys and Philip King. Colin and Philip are experienced teachers who have been involved in recent years with in-service training courses in music for primary colleagues. They are particularly concerned to enable those who call themselves "non-specialists" to engage in meaningful and exciting projects with their children. Colin has composed a number of works for children's voices, and Philip has worked extensively with choral projects and festivals.

Bible Societies exist to provide resources for Bible distribution and use. The British and Foreign Bible Society (BFBS) is a member of the United Bible Societies, an international partnership working in over 180 countries. Their common aim is to reach all people with the Bible, or some part of it, in a language they can understand and at a price they can afford. Parts of the Bible have now been translated into over 2000 languages. Bible Societies aim to help every church at every point where it uses the Bible. You are invited to share in this work by your prayers and gifts. The Bible Society in your country will be very happy to provide details of its activity.

CONTENTS

Acknowledgements — viii
Credits — x

Introduction to the Toolkit

General introduction — 3
Using the Toolkit — 5
Using the expressive arts in RE — 7
Concept cracking — 10
The three Es — 15
Exploring religious ideas — 16

I Art

Introduction

    Background — 21
    Resources — 22
    Art in the Bible — 23
    Biblical art — 24
    Twenty questions and activities — 26
    Talking pictures — 29
    Thirty-three art activities — 31

Detailed activities

    Banners — 35
    Calligrams — 36
    Stained glass — 37
    Marbling — 38
    Using a church — 39
    Collage — 40

Rubbings	41
Stolen picture	42
Water wash	45
Computer design	46
Book jackets	49
Mosaic	50
Calligraphy	51
Visual images	52
Wax resist	53
Wool wrapping	54
Masks	55
Diorama	56
Posters	57
Silhouettes and cameos	58
Cards	59
Printing	60
Costumes	62
Weaving	64
Symbols	65
Symbol dictionary	67

II Music

Introduction

Background	73
Resources	74
Assemblies and music	74
Ideas for listening	75
Music for different moods	76
Music in the Bible	78
Ten music activities	80

CONTENTS

Detailed activities

Procession	83
Musical stories (1)	86
Musical stories (2)	88
Singing project	90
Musical journeys	92
Rhythm (1)	95
Rhythm (2)	98
Rap	100
Soundscape (1)	105
Soundscape (2)	108
Sad stories, sad tunes	110
Joyful stories, joyful tunes	112
Musical characters	114
Chant	116
Carols	118
Psalms	121
Hymns	123
Spirituals	125
Jazz	129

Story index   133
Colour illustrations   139

ACKNOWLEDGEMENTS

I would like to express my thanks to the following people for their help in the writing of this book: Diane and Robin Walker, Deborah Helme, Ruth Cooper, Helen Thacker, Robert and Trevor Cooling. Ultimate responsibility for any errors is however mine alone. I would also like to thank Philip King and Colin Humphreys for contributing the Music section of *Art and Music Toolkit*.

My thanks to the following schools for their help in trialling material in these books:

Abbey Grange Church of England School, Leeds, West Yorkshire

Albany Junior School, Stapleford, Nottinghamshire

Belvoir High School, Nottingham

Bishop Ramsey Church of England School, Ruislip, Hillingdon, London

Bramcote Hills Primary School, Nottingham

Breadsall Hilltop Junior School, Derby

Brambletye Middle School, Redhill, Surrey

Brennands Endowed Primary School, Slaidburn, Clitheroe, Lancashire

Binscombe Middle School, Farncombe, Godalming, Surrey

Bishop John Robinson Primary School, Thamesmead, London

Coton Green Primary School, Tamworth, Staffordshire

Dovelands Junior School, Leicester

Fairfield Primary School, Stapleford, Nottinghamshire

George Spencer School, Stapleford, Nottinghamshire

Ifield Middle School, Crawley, West Sussex

Imberhorne School, East Grinstead, West Sussex

Kingswood (Wotton) County Primary School, Kingswood, Gloucestershire

ACKNOWLEDGEMENTS

Lowe's Wong Junior School, Southwell, Nottinghamshire

Lantern Lane Primary School, East Leake, Loughborough

Ladderbanks Middle School, Shipley, West Yorkshire

Myrtle Springs School, Sheffield

Newcastle-Under-Lyme School, Newcastle-Under-Lyme, Staffordshire

Nottingham High School for Girls, Nottinghamshire

Queen Elizabeth High School, Bromyard, Herefordshire

Robert Shaw Primary School, Aspley, Nottinghamshire

Rainey Endowed School, Magherafelt, Northern Ireland

St John's Church of England Primary School, Stapleford, Nottinghamshire

St Thomas à Becket High School, Sandal, Wakefield

St Peter's Church of England School, Cannock, Staffordshire

Sneinton Church of England Primary School, Sneinton, Nottinghamshire

Stevenson Junior School, Stapleford, Nottinghamshire

The Park School, Yeovil, Somerset

Ringwood School, Ringwood, Hampshire

These books have been produced under the auspices of the Stapleford Project. The Stapleford Project is a curriculum development initiative based at Stapleford House Education Centre. The project aims to produce materials and offer in-service training to resource the teaching of Christianity in schools. Stapleford House Education Centre is the national conference and study centre of the Association of Christian Teachers. Full details of courses and publications are available from: Stapleford House Education Centre, Wesley Place, Stapleford, Nottingham, NG9 8DP.

CREDITS

Every attempt has been made to trace and correctly attribute the sources of material within this book. Bible Society would gratefully receive any corrections for inclusion in future reprints.

	Page
Article on Incarnation from "RE Today", Volume 12 Number 1, Autumn 1994, reproduced by permission of Christian Education Movement, Royal Buildings, Victoria Street, Derby, DE1 1GW.	16
Adaptation of *Adam and Eve* © 1980 by Abubakar from *The Bible Through Asian Eyes* by Masao Takenaka and Ron O'Grady, reproduced by permission of Asian Christian Art Association, Japan.	24
Adaptation of drawing *Ruth* from the Misereor Lenten Veil *Biblical Women* painted by Lucy d'Souza © 1990, Misereor Medienproduktion und Vertriebsgesellschaft mbH, Aachen, Germany, used with permission.	24
Adaptation of *The annunciation* by Paul Woefel used by permission of the Gallery of Contemporary Art for Christian Books in Assisi.	25
Adaptation of painting *Last supper* by Jamini Roy (1887–1972) from *Christian Art in Asia* by Masao Takenaka, used with permission.	25
Adaptation of *Disciples asleep* by El Greco – original painting held by the National Gallery, London.	26
Adaptations of drawings of Christ child and shepherds' hands from Portinari altarpiece by Hugo van der Goes.	27, 32
Adaptation of *Christo scorto* by Andrea Mantegna held by the Pinacoteca di Brera, Milan.	28
Christ before the High Priest by Gerrit van Honthorst reproduced by courtesy of the Trustees, The National Gallery, London.	29
Adaptation of *Lamentations over dead Christ* mural by Giotto.	31
Illustration of dove adapted from *The annunciation* by Dante Gabriel Rossetti, held by the National Gallery, London.	33
Adaption of *Job* by James Daugherty. Reproduced by permission of the estate of James Daugherty, Courtesy of Salander-O'Reilly Galleries, New York.	33
The symbol dictionary adapted from *Saints, Signs and Symbols* by W Ellwood Post © SPCK 1964.	67

CREDITS

Let my people go traditional, arranged by Philip King and Colin Humphreys. — 89

Kum by ya traditional, arranged by Philip King and Colin Humphreys. — 92

The apostles rap by Philip King and Colin Humphreys. — 101

"O Come, O Come Emmanuel", melody adapted by Thomas Helmore (1811–90) from a French Missal. Words from *The Great O Antiphons* (12th–13th centuries); tr. John Mason Neale (1818–1866). Arranged by Sue Hatherly. — 117

"Nova, Nova" traditional. Taken from *Musica Britannica*, ed. J Stevens, Stainer and Bell, 1952. — 120

"Psalm 47", tune from Ravenscroft's seventeenth-century Psalter. Taken from *Stuart England* by A and M Bagenal, Longman, 1987. — 122

"Amazing Grace", tune Virginia Harmony, 1831. Words by John Newton. Arranged by Sue Hatherly. — 124

"Joshua fit the battle of Jericho", spiritual words and melody. Taken from *Alleluya*, ed. D Gadsby and J Hoggarth, A&C Black, 1980. — 127

"Oh when the Saints", traditional words and music. Arranged by Sue Hatherly. — 130

"Belshazzar's feast" by Rembrandt, reproduced by courtesy of the Trustees, The National Gallery, London. — 139

Motifs V, VI, VII and VIII from the Misereor Lenten Veil from Ethiopia painted by Alemayehu Bizuneh © 1978, Misereor Medienproduktion und Vertriebsgesellschaft mbH, Aachen, Germany, used with permission. — 140

The annunciation by Dante Gabriel Rossetti reproduced by courtesy of The Tate Gallery, London. — 141

The plumbline and the city © Judges Postcards Ltd. of Hastings, used with permission. — 142

INTRODUCTION TO THE TOOLKIT

GENERAL INTRODUCTION

This series of three books is designed for teachers who want ready access to a wide range of teaching activities for exploring the Bible in the classroom. Each book covers two subject areas and has been written with the non-specialist in mind. The activities are appropriate for both primary and secondary schools and they have been designed for use with the 7–14 age group. However, many of them are "ageless" and can be used with a much wider age range.

The three books cover the following six areas.

Writing / Poetry } Book 1   Story / Drama } Book 2   Art / Music } Book 3

These books concentrate on method; they do not constitute a systematic curriculum. The stories used to illustrate each activity are meant only as examples. Teachers are encouraged to apply these activities to the biblical material within their own syllabuses. They should not feel that the application of the activities is restricted to the biblical examples given in these books.

Biblical stories

Usually between two and four Bible stories are given to illustrate each activity. They are the type of material on which the activity in question works well. Full textual references are given, but teachers are not expected to use all of these. For example, if a story appears in all four Gospels, all four references are usually given so that the teacher can choose which account they prefer. The references are based on the Good News version unless indicated otherwise.

Teachers may not wish to use all of a biblical story suggested – some contain parts which are unsuitable for young children: for example with younger children the story of Jericho is best ended before the massacre. Biblical stories are often better retold by the teacher or read from a modern retelling of the stories rather than directly from the text. Information on relevant books can be found on page 23, *Story and Drama Toolkit*.

Health and safety

As with any subject, all activities and materials used in RE should be safe, this particularly applies to art materials.

Examples of pupil work

Pupil work has been included where appropriate. Different numbering systems for year groups are used in various parts of the British Isles. Most of the pupil work in this book comes from England and Northern Ireland where the following numbering systems are used.

England
Year 3 (7–8), Year 4 (8–9), Year 5 (9–10), Year 6 (10–11), Year 7 (11–12), Year 8 (12–13), Year 9 (13–14).

Northern Ireland
P4 (7–8), P5 (8–9), P6 (9–10), P7 (10–11), Year 1 (11–12), Year 2 (12–13), Year 3 (13–14).

Pupil work representing a full ability range has been used. It can be depressing for teachers to see only work by the most able pupils! The pupil work in this book is not always accurate, as it has been created by pupils with a wide age and ability range. Such inaccuracies have been retained for the sake of authenticity.

Abbreviations used

Unless otherwise stated, biblical quotations are from the Good News Bible. Otherwise the following abbreviations are used to indicate the version of the Bible being quoted.

AV   Authorized Version
RSV   Revised Standard Version
NIV   New International Version

Photocopying

The material in this book is not photocopiable unless specifically indicated on the relevant page. Photocopies may only be made for use within the purchasing institution.

USING THE TOOLKIT

Subject areas

Each book in this series covers two subject areas: for example, story and drama. Each area is presented in two chapters, the first introducing the subject area and the second detailing activities.

The first, introductory chapter will contain at least the following four sections.

1. Background. A brief introduction to how the subject area can be used to explore the Bible.

2. Resource List. A list of general resources on the subject area.

3. The place of the subject area in the Bible. A brief exploration of the place of the subject area in the Bible, for example, drama in the Bible.

4. Numbered activities. These sections bear headings such as "Thirty art activities" and present brief descriptions of activities for the classroom which are not elaborated in detail.

The second chapter contains a number of detailed descriptions of activities showing how they can be applied to example Bible stories.

Each section detailing an activity is laid out as follows.

- Bible stories with references
- Description of the activity
- Examples of pupil work (where applicable)
- Biblical application

Selecting appropriate activities

Teachers can select in two ways.

Either: Look up the story you wish to teach in the story index at the back of the book and select from the activities which use that story as an example. So, if you wish to teach the story of the Prodigal Son, you will find activities using this story on pages 31, 39, 55, *Writing and Poetry Toolkit*.

Or: Decide on the subject area you would like to use. For example, you might decide you want to teach the parable of the Prodigal Son and you would like to use a writing activity. Look through the writing activities and select any activity you think suits the story, the time you have available, and the pupils you teach. It does not matter if the story you wish to tell does not occur in the examples. For example, to teach the Prodigal Son you might select "Letters and Postcards" on page 39, *Writing and Poetry Toolkit*.

IMPORTANT NOTE: Classifying activities is difficult, for some work equally well as poetry, writing, or drama. Many poetry activities work well as prose and vice versa. Story activities such as "Conversations" also work well as drama. Teachers are advised, therefore, not to restrict themselves to one area, as there may be appropriate activities which can be adapted from other subject areas.

USING THE EXPRESSIVE ARTS IN RE

The expressive arts have a long association with the Christian faith and still play an important part in Christian life and worship. Despite the occasional period of iconoclasm, Christians have used the arts as a means of expressing faith and worship in forms as diverse as icon, church architecture, and the novel. The writers of the Bible themselves utilized the expressive arts in, for example, poetry, story, song, the drama of ritual and prophetic action.

In the classroom the role of the arts is not just to decorate pieces of work or enliven lessons, but to encourage pupils to explore Christianity and express their own ideas. Of course, the arts may enliven a lesson or decorate a piece of work, but that is not their prime function.

Content and meaning

The focus of the majority of activities in these books is the exploration of the meaning and significance of biblical material. A smaller number of the activities are designed for mastering its content. However, content and meaning should not be considered to be mutually exclusive: content has to be mastered in order that significance can be explored in depth. Expression without research, creativity without content can lead to superficial work: both are needed for successful learning.

Skills versus expression

The teaching of specific skills, such as poetry activities, may be seen as an unnecessary curtailing of the pupils' freedom to express themselves. However, this should not be seen as an "either–or" choice. The skills are essential as they are the means by which the pupils are freed to express themselves. Some techniques, by restricting a child to a specific range of tasks, actually enable the pupil to explore the subject matter in a depth they would be unlikely to achieve if left to their own devices. For example, the restriction to a set number of syllables in Haiku writing forces the pupil to choose words very carefully.

Active and passive learning

In discussion of teaching methods the following is often considered to be true:

$$\text{Good} = \text{active} = \text{informal}$$

$$\text{Bad} = \text{passive} = \text{formal}$$

Such categories are too simplistic. A good learning activity is one which engages pupils so that they become involved with the subject matter. A poor learning activity is one which fails to engage them.

If we wish to describe good learning activities as "active" ones, it must be remembered that "active" need not necessarily mean physically active. The key characteristic of successful active learning is that the pupil is engaged by the content. For example, it is quite possible for pupils to be physically active in a drama "acting out" a story but never engage with it. On the other hand pupils can listen to a well-told story without being physically active whilst being totally engaged at the level of mind and emotion.

Good teaching can be formal and physically passive as long as it stimulates pupils to reprocess the information and use the insights they have acquired, expressing them in their own way.

Conversation

A lot of good RE happens in conversation and time for talk needs to be built into activities. Many of the activities in these books will only work at a shallow level, if pupils are not given time to discuss the ideas involved with either their peers or their teacher. The classroom may be the only place in which pupils are able to discuss religious issues. Many inhabit an otherwise secular world in which talk of God would be a conversation stopper.

Many of the activities in this book act as conversation starters. For example, during trialling, the senses activity on page 105 of *Writing and Poetry Toolkit* led to a surprisingly profound conversation on the nature of God.

The limits of the arts in RE

There should be limits to the use of the arts in RE, not because they do not work but because they can be too effective! It is important to be sensitive, and some activities ought not to be used with certain material. For example, it would be quite inappropriate to enter into a graphic retelling of the crucifixion story which focused on the horrors of this method of execution.

There are times when methods which provide more distance from the material are needed, for example using puppets, video, "formal" writing activities, rather than the "involvement in" type of activity.

Respecting pupil integrity

When exploring a biblical story, it is important to be sensitive towards the pupils' own beliefs (or lack of them) and the faith commitment of their families. The most effective way of achieving this is to use what is called "owning and grounding" language. This means that we always speak of a particular Bible story as belonging to the Christian religion. For example, stories can be introduced with statements such as, "Today we are going to look at a story which is very important to Christians". Christian beliefs should be prefaced with a phrase such as "Christians believe" rather than inclusive language such as "We all …" or "You should …". This allows pupils the freedom to identify with the story if they are Christians, or to explore it from another standpoint if they are not.

I have retained the terms BC, AD and Old Testament as these are the terms used by the Christian community and this is a book about the Christian Bible. Teachers may wish to change these terms to BCE, CE and Hebrew Bible.

CONCEPT CRACKING

This is a planning process developed by the Stapleford Project which aims to bring out the central ideas contained in a Bible story or belief. Those ideas can then be explored using the arts. The process can be broken down into four main stages using the mnemonic U-S-E-R. It can be used to develop a structure for one lesson or activity, or for a series of lessons, or a unit of work. By emphasizing one main route through a story, theme or festival, it allows you to revisit stories and emphasize other aspects at another date.

Concept cracking an idea: forgiveness

*Stage 1: **Unpack the idea***
Example: What is forgiveness really about? Forgiveness is about being sorry; it is about changing for the better when you have been forgiven. It is not exacting revenge when you have a right to "get your own back".

*Stage 2: **Select one main idea from the many ideas to follow up***
Example: Changing for the better after being forgiven.

*Stage 3: **Engage with the pupils' experience***
Example: This can be done by directly drawing on the pupils' experience or in other ways, such as through fiction – for example, the story of how Eustace changed in *The Voyage of the Dawn Treader* by C S Lewis.

*Stage 4: **Religious and Relevant***
Introduce the religious material and make it relevant.
Example: Tell one or more stories of forgiveness and change such as Zacchaeus (Luke 19.1–10) and Jesus' story of the Two Debtors (Luke 7.36–50). (See pages 27–30, *Story and Drama* for more). Explore these stories with the pupils using activities such as "Diorama" on page 56, and "Close ups" page 31.

Relevance
Show the story's relevance for modern Christians today. Tell a modern story of a person who was forgiven and who showed by the way they behaved that they had changed.

Suggest ways the story can have relevance for all. This should be done in such a way that pupils are free to find personal relevance in the story if they wish. Example: think quietly for a moment about times when you have been sorry and how you showed that you had changed.

Stages 1 and 2 are initial teacher planning stages. The pupils' first learning experience is of something which is relevant to them at stage 3. Further ideas for stories and themes which can be used at stage 4 of the planning process can be found on pages 27–30, *Story and Drama*.

Examples follow of how this same approach can be used on a single story such as Ruth or on a festival such as Christmas.

Concept cracking a story: Ruth

*Stage 1: **U**npack the idea*
The story of Ruth is about commitment and God's care in adversity. It's a story of love and faithfulness.

*Stage 2: **S**elect one idea to follow up*
Example: Commitment.

*Stage 3: **E**ngage with the pupils' experience*
Talk about the pupils' commitment to their friends.
When is loyalty difficult?

*Stage 4: **R**eligious and relevant*
Introduce the biblical material and make it relevant.
Tell the story of Ruth. Explore it using techniques such as "Printing" page 60.

Relevance
Relate a modern story of Christian commitment or explore the marriage service.
   Ask pupils to think about people to whom they are committed.

Concept cracking a festival: Christmas

With a festival, there is one stage prior to unpacking – this can be likened to creating a "jigsaw". If a festival is imagined to be like a jigsaw picture, made up of many parts, then a different piece of the "jigsaw" can be covered each year. Examples of jigsaws for Christmas, Easter, Pentecost and Harvest are given overleaf.

Christmas

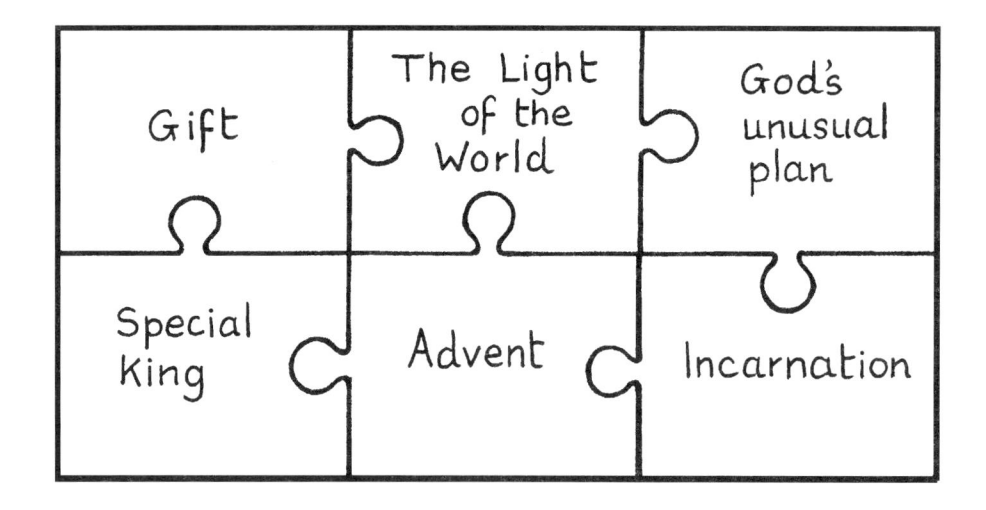

```
┌──────────┬──────────┬──────────┐
│          │ The Light│  God's   │
│   Gift   │  of the  │ unusual  │
│          │  World   │   plan   │
├──────────┼──────────┼──────────┤
│ Special  │          │          │
│  King    │  Advent  │Incarnation│
│          │          │          │
└──────────┴──────────┴──────────┘
```

Gift (God's gift of Jesus – John 3.16; the wise men's gifts – Matthew 2.11)

The light of the world (John 1.9; 8.12; 12.35–36)

God's unusual plan (God's choice of a poor couple in an occupied land)

The special king (Messiah – Isaiah 9.1–7; 11.1–9; Luke 1.67–79)

Advent (waiting in hope, prophecy – Isaiah 7.14; Micah 5.2)

Incarnation (Immanuel "God with us" – Matthew 1.18–23, Hebrews 4.15–16)

Easter

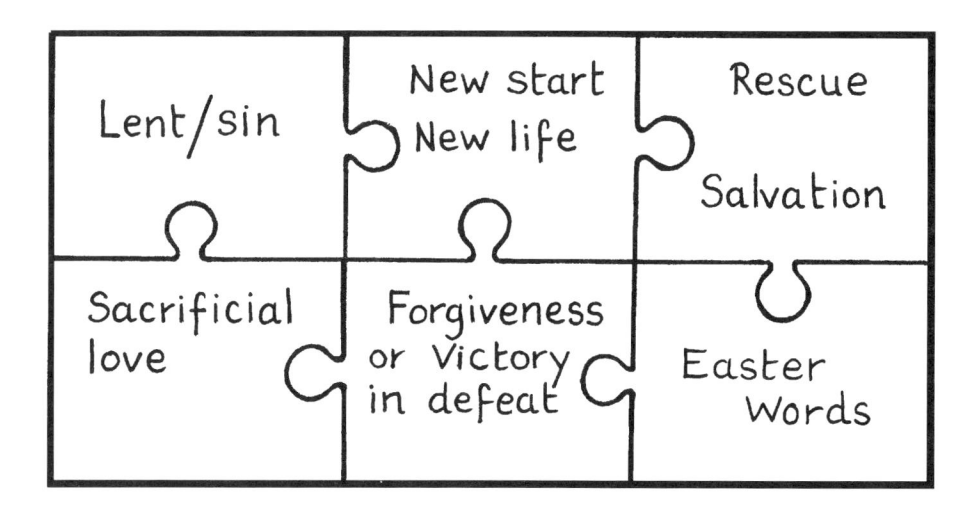

```
┌──────────┬──────────┬──────────┐
│          │ New start│  Rescue  │
│ Lent/sin │ New life │          │
│          │          │ Salvation│
├──────────┼──────────┼──────────┤
│Sacrificial│Forgiveness│         │
│  love    │or Victory│  Easter  │
│          │in defeat │  Words   │
└──────────┴──────────┴──────────┘
```

Lent (preparation for Easter, spiritual spring-clean)

New start, new life (life-out-of-death symbolism; people who started a new life after meeting Jesus)

Sin (the adulterous woman – John 8.1–11, all have done wrong) (older pupils)

Rescue, salvation (Noah as an example of rescue; Jesus rescues from sin)

INTRODUCTION TO THE TOOLKIT

Forgiveness (Jesus on the cross, the dying thief)

Victory in defeat (resurrection after death)

Sacrificial love (dying for others)

Easter words ("atonement" – covering or erasing wrong, and similar)

Pentecost (celebrating the Holy Spirit)

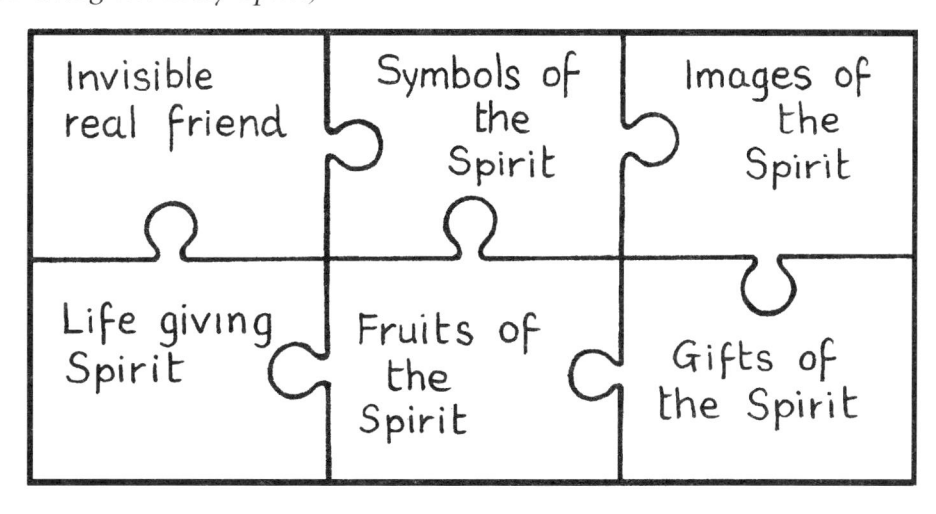

Invisible real friend	Symbols of the Spirit	Images of the Spirit
Life giving Spirit	Fruits of the Spirit	Gifts of the Spirit

An invisible but real friend (John 14.25–27)

The symbols of the Holy Spirit (wind, fire – Acts 2; dove – Matthew 3.13–17)

The images of the Holy Spirit (comforter, counsellor – John 14.16; 15.26)

The gifts of the Spirit (1 Corinthians 12)

The fruits of the Spirit (Galatians 5.22, 23)

Life-giving Spirit (Genesis 1.2; 2.7; Ezekiel 37.1–14; John 3.1–21)

Harvest

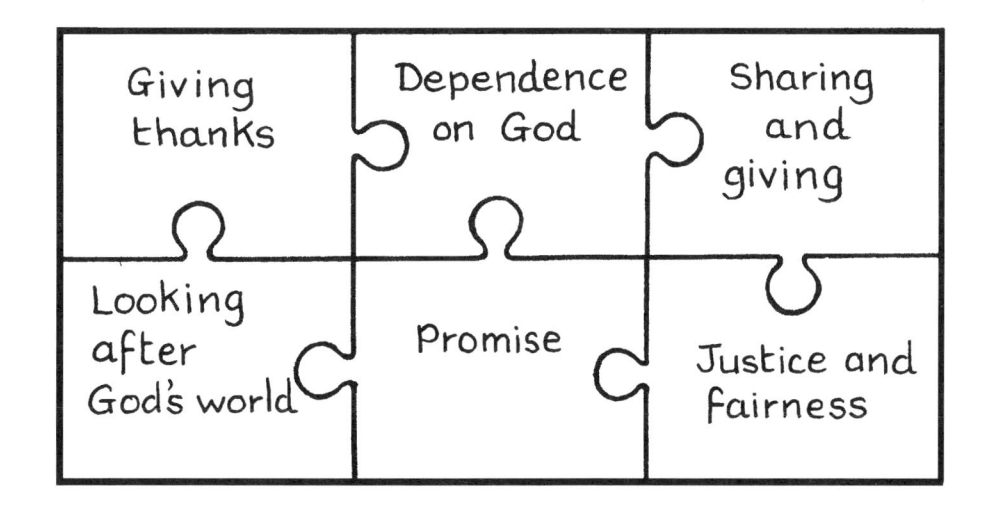

Giving thanks	Dependence on God	Sharing and giving
Looking after God's world	Promise	Justice and fairness

Giving thanks (Psalm 136.1–9; the story of the ten lepers – Luke 17.11–19)

Dependence on God (God the provider – the Israelites in the wilderness – Exodus 16.1–36)

Sharing and giving (the story of Ruth – Book of Ruth; the widow's gift – Luke 21.1–4; the rich fool – Luke 12.13–21)

Looking after God's world (creation – Genesis 1 and 2)

Promise (Noah – Genesis 8.22)

Justice and fairness (inequalities in sharing; relief agencies; biblical laws on just treatment of the poor – Deuteronomy 10.19; 15.7; 24.17; Luke 14.13; James 5.1–5)

Where a festival is based on a particular story, the whole story will be told each time but a different aspect will be highlighted each year. Approaching festivals in this way ensures both continuity and progression as the students' understanding develops over the years of schooling. Having prepared the jigsaw the concept cracking methodology is then applied to the particular piece of the jigsaw to be taught. An example follows.

Christmas: God's unusual plan

*Stage 1: **Unpack the idea***
The choice of Mary. Jesus born into a poor Jewish family.
The poor circumstances of the birth. Making plans.

*Stage 2: **Select one idea to follow up***
The choice of Mary.

*Stage 3: **Engage with the pupils' experience***
Give the pupils the opportunity to make choices and ask them to justify why they chose as they did.

*Stage 4: **Religious and relevant***
Introduce biblical material and make it relevant.
Tell the story of the annunciation. Use the "Stolen picture" activity on page 42, *Art and Music* for this. Other biblical characters who were not obvious choices can be explored: Gideon, David, Moses, Jeremiah.

Relevance
Look at the life of a modern Christian such as Mother Teresa. Would they have been an obvious choice?

Ask pupils to think about their own choices. Do they always make the obvious choices? Do they need to look closer at people and see the hidden potential?

A booklet entitled *Concept Cracking: Exploring Christian Beliefs in Schools* giving further details of this process is available from Stapleford House, Wesley Place, Stapleford, Notts. NG9 8DP.

THE THREE Es

When using activities from these books, it is important to be clear about their purpose. Activities have three roles:

- To engage. They engage a pupil's interest and earth the subject in the child's world.
- To explore. They help pupils explore the meaning and significance of a subject.
- To express. They help pupils express their own understanding of a subject after due exploration.

Sometimes an activity can have more than one purpose. Here is an example of how one activity can be used to fulfil the three different purposes.

- Engage. Give the pupils three faces from a local newspaper, then ask them to select one face and say what may have happened to create the expression (choose with care).
- Explore. To explore the story of Moses and the bulrushes, give the pupils the three faces below. Tell the pupils they are all the same character. Ask them to suggest which character it is, what each face expresses, and why the character feels that way.
- Express. Give the pupils freedom to choose any character from the story at any moment. Ask them to draw or describe what they think that person's expression would be and why they felt that way.

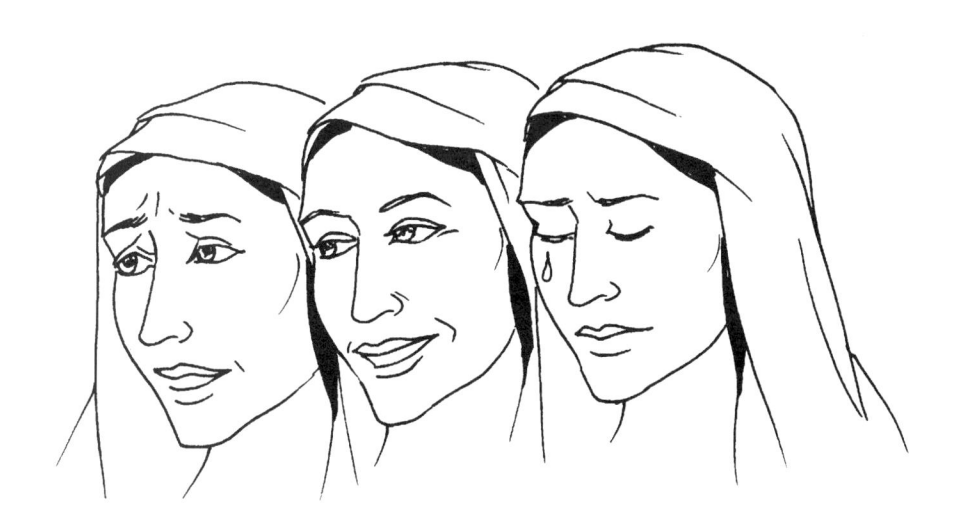

EXPLORING RELIGIOUS IDEAS

The arts can be used to explore religious ideas which are often thought of as too difficult for children. The expressive nature of the arts means they can often carry ideas that are beyond analysis intellectually. Through dance, art, and poetry, pupils can "catch a feel" of things they may not fully understand. For example, the central belief in the Christmas story is called INCARNATION – a big word which understandably deters most teachers. Some of the ideas contained within this Christian belief are:

God with us (Matthew 1.23; Hebrews 4.15–16)

The incarnation (the word literally means "in flesh") is God's son becoming one of us. It has been described as "God with skin on"! The word Immanuel simply means "God with us". It is God's son sharing human life, knowing what it is like to be human: what it means to laugh and to cry, to have friends and to be rejected. As a result of this doctrine, Christians believe people can pray feeling confident they will be understood, as Jesus knows the trials and joys of being human.

Giving up power (Philippians 2.5–9)

Becoming one of us meant giving up power and control. It meant facing poverty and danger. It was the creator becoming part of his own creation. (Christians believe Jesus, God, and the Holy Spirit were all involved in creation.)

The purpose of the incarnation (John 3.16)

The purpose of the incarnation was to rescue or save. Christians see Jesus as a baby with a mission, someone who came to change the situation and show people what God is like by his teaching and the way he lived.

Ways of exploring the incarnation using the arts

- The idea of giving up power
  Explore what it would be like for the teacher or head teacher to start in the infants. What would s/he have to give up? What would s/he miss? This can be done verbally as a discussion, as an interview, or as a written exercise. Christians believe that Jesus is God's son and gave up many things to come to earth to share our lives.

- Giving up control

    The incarnation is the creator becoming part of his own creation. It is an author becoming part of his or her own book, subject to the plot and all the conditions that prevail within the story. An author is outside the story, in control, safe. A character is not safe: they can be in danger, as Jesus was. Look through some story books with the pupils and decide which character they would be if "sucked" into the book. What conditions would they have to endure? What dangers would they be in? Christians believe Jesus willingly became part of his own creation because he loved people. He became part of our story, subject to its dangers. This can be done as a storytelling or writing activity.

- The creator becoming part of his own creation

    This can be done visually through art. Use dark frieze paper and create a night sky with stars, planets, and so on. In the heart of this, paint a crib scene, or use the night sky as the background to the nativity figures. Underneath have the words of a carol such as "Lo, within a manger lies he who made the starry skies" from "See amid the winter's snow".

- What it's like to be me

    Pupils can write about themselves and try to communicate "What it is like to be me". Give the pupils specific items to write about, so that it is not too intrusive: likes, hates, what it is like to be ten years old, for example. The incarnation is about "God in our shoes". Christians believe God's son became one of us and understands what it is like to be human, and that therefore he understands when people pray.

- Being human

    Christians believe Jesus knew what it was like to be human but with one important exception: he did no wrong. He knew what it was like to be tempted, to laugh, and to cry. These emotions can be communicated in dance or drama, or simple masks can be used made from paper plates showing the different expressions.

- Sharing

    We can share many things – money, time, toys. Pupils can play sharing games, or talk about the different things that can be shared. Christians believe that God shared what was most important to him – his son. They believe that Jesus shared our human life and knows what it is like to be human.

- Purpose

    Pupils can explore the idea of having a special mission. This can be done in the "secret agent" role-play format. The pupils become the agents who are given all sorts of missions on slips of paper by the teacher or leader. When the leader of the meeting has left, the agents get together to discuss who has the most difficult mission before they leave to start their assignments. Christians believe Jesus came with a special, very difficult, mission, to show people what God is like. He did this by the things he taught, and by the way he lived and died.

- The most special baby

    Young pupils can start by contrasting special and ordinary. Create a special display: special clothes, objects, toys. Talk about special people. For Christians, Jesus was the most special baby ever because they believe he was God's son.

ART

INTRODUCTION

Background

Christianity has an artistic history stretching back to the earliest days when Christians drew on the walls of the catacombs. Christians have always expressed their faith in art, from stained glass to sculpture, from mosaic to illuminated manuscripts. Some art forms have a teaching role; others express personal or corporate faith or help to lift believers in worship.

At various times, Christians have reacted against art, and many works of art were lost. This happened in the eighth century and again in the seventeenth century in some Protestant countries. On the whole, the attitude towards art has been positive and the Church was a great patron of art. Indeed, many major works of art are still to be found in religious houses or churches though some are now housed in galleries.

In schools, art can have a major role to play in RE:

- It is non-verbal and allows a range of pupils to express themselves. For some pupils, this will be a freeing experience; for others, their lack of skills will be frustrating. Time spent on basic skills is never wasted; it frees pupils to express what they want to say.
- Art allows pupils to become involved, to a greater or lesser degree, with the material. In RE this is both an asset and a danger. Art allows pupils to explore at depth, but pupil integrity needs protecting. See page 9.
- The process of creating encourages pupils to respond. This is particularly important in RE, which has an "affective" (feeling) dimension as well as academic content. Pupils should be free to respond in a way appropriate for them.
- The choices which are part of the creative process involve pupils in evaluation and decision making – a vital part of RE.
- Art involves awareness which can lead to understanding. Without this awareness, RE can be a dry, intellectual exercise. It may result in the awareness that the belief under exploration is an important one for Christians, or it may be a more personal response. Both are acceptable responses in RE.

When art is used in RE, full weight should be given to the meaning of the events depicted, the roles characters fulfil, and the significance of the story. In the activity section, there are many suggestions for techniques which can be used to explore biblical stories, but the purpose is not just to create accurate backdrops or a faithfully reproduced picture. By use of colour, texture, and technique, something of the meaning of the event should be communicated. By the way a person is depicted, their feelings, character and role can be portrayed. Inevitably some techniques, by their nature, are more suited to recording "content" and others more suited to capturing mood and meaning. Whatever type of activity is used, significance should be kept uppermost. Often meaning can be explored informally by the teacher asking questions: "Why choose that colour?", "What position would the person be in?", "Why?", "Where would they be looking?"

ART

Resources

Books

NOTE: Some of these are out of print but are available through libraries.

Christian art

Folens Art Pack: Christianity by E Baker (Folens, 1995)
A Child's Book of Prayer in Art by Sister Wendy Beckett (Dorling Kindersley, 1995)
The Bible in Art: Old Testament by R Muhleberger (New York, Moore and Moore Publishing, 1991)
Modern Art in English Churches by M Day (Mowbray, 1984)
Stained Glass: An Illustrated History by S Brown (Studio Editions, 1992)
Rose Windows by P Cowen (Thames and Hudson, 1979)
The Bible and its Painters by Bruce Bernard (MacDonald and Co Ltd, 1983)
Christian Art book and video, Arlosh Educational Resources (The Farmington Institute). (Secondary)
The Illustrated Life of Jesus Christ by J Rhymer (Bloomsbury Publishing, 1991)
Angels by C Johnson (Fount, 1993)
A Colouring Book of the New Testament (through manuscript illuminations) (Bellerophon Books, 1988)
A Colouring Book of the Old Testament (through manuscript illuminations) (Bellerophon Books, 1991)
Ancient Irish Art (Celtic art) (Bellerophon Books, 1990)
The Middle Ages (an alphabet of illuminated lettering) (Bellerophon Books, 1991)
* *The Bible Through Asian Eyes* by Masao Takenaka and Ron O'Grady (Pace Publishing/Asian Christian Art Association, 1991)
* *Immanuel, The Coming of Jesus in Art and the Bible* by Hans Ruedi Weber (Eerdmans/World Council of Churches, 1984)
* *Christian Art in Asia* by Masao Takenaka (Kyo Bun Kwan/Christians Conference of Asia, 1975)

* See also the section on "biblical art" (pages 24–25).

NOTE: The two colouring books contain beautiful black and white drawings which can be cut up for display. They do not have to be used as colouring books. Bellerophon Books are available from St Anne's Music Society, 8 Collingham Gardens, London, SW5 0HW.

General

Influential Artists by E Baker (Folens, 1992)
What is Art? by R Davidson (OUP, 1993)
Children's Art and the Computer by K Mathieson (Hodder & Stoughton, 1993)
Art, Craft and Design in the Primary School edited by J Lancaster (National Society for Education in Art and Design, 1990)
Inspirations for Art by P Kenyon and T Reynolds (Scholastic, 1993)
Active Art 1 and 2 by R Fisher (Simon & Schuster, 1994)
Start with Art by S Fitzsimmons (Simon & Schuster, 1991)
Art 4-11 by M Morgan (Simon & Schuster, 1991)
Teaching Painting in the Primary School by K Gentle (Cassell, 1993)
Principles and Practice in Art by R Clement and S Page (Oliver & Boyd, 1992)
Knowledge and Understanding in Art by R Clement and S Page (Oliver & Boyd, 1992)
Investigating and Making in Art by R Clement and S Page (Oliver & Boyd, 1992)
Approaches to Art; Teacher's Resource Book by A Peppin, R Smith, and A Turner (Ginn, 1992)
Approaches to Art: Teacher's Resource Book Key Stage 2 by A Peppin, R Smith and A Turner (Ginn, 1993)
The Story of Painting by Sister Wendy Beckett (Dorling Kindersley, 1994)
Looking at Paintings by J Welton (Dorling Kindersley, 1994)
A Work of Art by J Chambers et al. (Belair, 1995)

INTRODUCTION

Art in the Bible

The second commandment, to make no graven image, meant that painting and sculpture, particularly of the human form, was not developed in Israel. It was feared this would lead to idolatry. To date, no such sculpture has been found which is definitely Hebrew.

The Israelites were not unappreciative of art, but it is often difficult to distinguish Hebrew art from that of close neighbours such as the inhabitants of Phoenicia (modern Lebanon) and Canaan (Palestine).

The Israelites were quick to learn from their neighbours, however. The Phoenicians had skill in dyeing cloth; the Philistines worked with iron.

Pottery was developed in Palestine, the fast wheel being in use as early as 3,000 BC. The prophet Jeremiah gives a picture of the potter at work in Jeremiah 18.

The Israelites had enough skill to cast and carve a golden calf in the desert (Exodus 32.2–4) and men such as Bezalel were skilled in working in metal, wood, and embroidery. Israelites were highly skilled at embroidery, which was used on both men's and women's clothing (Ezekiel 16.18; 26.16; Psalm 45.14). The designs for the Tabernacle and the High Priests' robes detail exquisite patterning (Exodus 35.30–33).

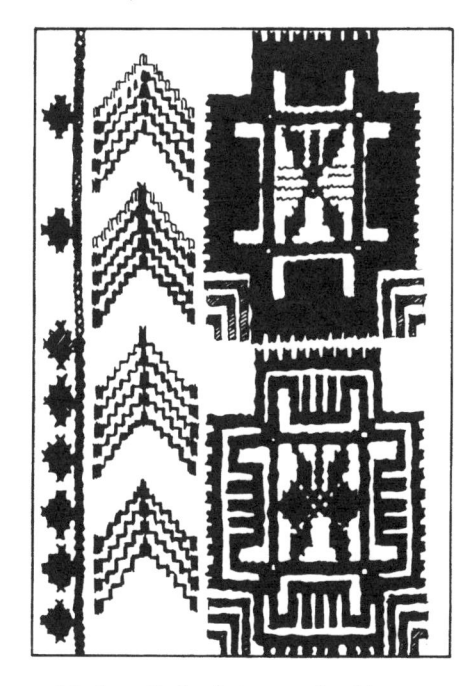

Modern Palestinian embroidery

Under David and Solomon, Phoenician artists were brought in to train Israelite craftsmen. The resulting description of the Temple shows that the Israelites did not lack artistic creativity, though again it is difficult to distinguish what was Israelite and what was Phoenician.

The Israelites, in common with their neighbours, may have painted directly onto plaster, though few examples have been found. Wood carving was developed: the Temple was decorated with carved wooden flowers, palm leaves and cherubim. Domestic furniture was also beautifully carved and came in for condemnation by the prophets – not because they were against art, but the materials used were so expensive that it meant some were living in luxury while others starved (Jeremiah 22.14; Haggai 1.4).

Ivory and bone were used for carving, either free-standing or inlaid in wood, and the Israelites may have developed great skill in using metal. In the Temple, there stood a huge bowl cast as a bronze "sea". It rested on the backs of twelve cast oxen.

Carpenters, potters and stonemasons made the everyday things of life, but also carved and beautified them. Carpenters made farm implements and beautifully carved wooden bowls. Metal workers made metal farm implements and also delicate bronze work and jewellery. Stonemasons made cornerstones for houses. (Houses made entirely of stone were rare as stone was expensive.) They were also able to construct Herod's Temple, cutting the blocks of stone so accurately that they fitted together without mortar, and to this day it is still impossible to insert a knife blade between the remaining stones.

ART

Biblical art

Making any list of biblical art is fraught with difficulties. The lists below largely consist of paintings, although there are myriad forms of biblical art which this excludes. The reason for this narrow focus is a practical one. Books with reproductions of paintings are easily available through libraries, and paintings can often be bought in postcard form from galleries, whereas books on biblical sculpture, stained glass, and tapestry are less easily available. The paintings below reflect biblical subject matter. Inclusion does not necessarily mean the painters were Christian, neither does it deal with that broader range of art which reflects biblical ideas if not subject matter.

Creation
The earthly paradise, Jacopo Bassano
Creation, Abraham Walkowitz
* *In the beginning,* Egai Fernandez

An adaption of Abubakar's Adam and Eve

Temptation
Adam and Eve under the apple tree, Edvard Munch
* *Adam and Eve,* Abubakar

Noah
The deluge, John Martin
Noah and the flood, Alemayehu Bizuneh [2]
The ark of Noah, Solomon Raj

Patriarchs
* *The sacrifice of Isaac,* He Huibing
Abraham and the three angels, Gaudenzio Ferrari

Jacob's dream, J M W Turner
Jacob receiving Joseph's blood-stained coat, Diego Velázquez
Joseph making himself known to his brothers, Marc Chagall

Moses
The finding of Moses, Frederick Dillon
* *The burning bush,* Paul Koli
Moses receiving the tablets of the Law, Marc Chagall

David
* *David and Saul,* He Qi
David, Michelangelo
David and Goliath, Edgar Degas

Prophets, Heroes, and Heroines
Samson and Delilah, Valerio Castello
* *Ruth and Naomi,* Yoshihei Miya
Ruth, Naomi, and Boaz, Lucy d'Souza [2]
The peaceable kingdom (Isaiah 11.6), Edward Hicks
Jonah, Albert Pinkham Ryder
* *Jonah,* Sadao Watanabe
Daniel in the lions' den, Henry Ossawa Tanner
Belshazzar sees the writing on the wall, Rembrandt van Rijn
Job, James Daugherty
Esther denouncing Haman, Ernest Normand

An adaption of Lucy d' Souza's drawing of Ruth

Jesus' birth
* *The annunciation,* Paul Woelfel
Madonna and child, Henry Moore

INTRODUCTION

Madonna and child, Maureen Colpman
Armenian Infancy Cycle [1]
* *Flight into Egypt*, Francis Sekitoleko

An adaption of an angel from Paul Woefel's
Annunciation

Jesus' childhood
Christ in the house of his parents, John Everett Millais
Finding the saviour in the temple, W Holman Hunt

Ministry of Jesus
The Life of Christ according to Chinese Artists (SPCK) [3]
* *The baptism*, Constance Stokes
Christ in the wilderness, Stanley Spencer
Christ's temptation, Jacques Chery [2]
Christ blessing children, Nicolaes Maes
Kitchen scene with Christ in the house with Mary and Martha, Diego Velázquez
Zacchaeus, Alemayehu Bizuneh [2]
The transfiguration, Raphael

Miracles of Jesus
The marriage feast at Cana, Bartholomé-Esteban Murillo
The raising of Jairus's daughter, George Percy Jacomb-Hood
Christ walking on the water, Alessandro Magnasco

Christ's teaching
* *The prodigal son*, Thomas Chelladurai
* *Ten virgins*, Yoshie Kawakami
* *The good Samaritan*, Kim Ki-Chang
The light of the world, W Holman Hunt

Last events of Jesus' life
Christ washing Peter's feet, Ford Madox Brown
Christ driving the money-changers from the Temple, El Greco
* *The Last Supper*, Jamini Roy
The agony in the garden, Andrea Mantegna
* *Judas*, Hong Chong Myung
Christ before Caiaphas, Gerrit van Honthorst
The betrayal, Mark Cazalet
Christ carrying the cross, Stanley Spencer
* *Simon of Cyrene helps Christ carry the cross*, Miriam Rose Ungurmerr
The crucifixion, Salvador Dali
* *The crucifixion*, Kim Yong Gil
The resurrection, Piero della Francesca
Mary Magdalene and the disciples, Lucy D'Souza [2]
Armenian Easter cycle [1]
* *The ascension*, Bagong Kussudiardja
* *Pentecost*, Tadao Tanaka

An adaption of the disciples from Jamini Roy's
Last Supper

(1) These are available in large poster form from St Paul Multimedia Productions UK, Middle Green, Slough, SL3 6BS.
(2) The work of these artists is available on large printed cloths from Cafod, 2 Romero Close, Stockwell, London SW9 9TY or from Misereor, Mozartstrasse 9, 5100 Aachen, Germany.
(3) At present out of print, but available through libraries.
* The work of these artists is available in the three books marked with a star in the resources section page 22. They can be purchased through the World Council of Churches, 150 Route de Ferney, 1211 Geneva 20, Switzerland.

ART

Twenty questions and activities

There are a number of general questions which can be asked of any work of art, whether it is religious or not. The questions and activities below apply to paintings on biblical subjects, but a similar set could be devised for sculpture, stained glass, and so on. A detailed list of paintings with biblical subjects is given on pages 24–25.

(1) What is the story? What are we looking at?
Pupils can write their own story of a picture, or give a written or oral description. This can be done before or after researching the biblical story behind a picture such as the painting of Belshazzar's feast (page 139).

(2) What is the title of the picture? Does the title help you to understand the painting?
Give the pupils a number of paintings on biblical subjects but without their titles. Ask them to invent titles which will not only describe the picture but also help people to understand it.

(3) What are the people doing in the picture?
Give each group a painting or postcard. Ask each member of the group to choose one person from the painting and describe what is happening to them or what they are doing.

(4) What do you think will happen next?
Ask pupils to treat the pictures as the paused frame of a video, and predict what was about to happen next. Press fast forward.

(5) What has just occurred?
Do the reverse of the activity above. What has just occurred to create this scene? Press rewind.

(6) Has the painting got a message?
Not all messages are written. Art often contains a message in the way the people and places are painted, the colours and symbols used, and the arrangement of the picture. Look closely at the painting, has it got a message? Read a biblical story with the pupils. What is the meaning or message of the story. How could that message be conveyed by art?

(7) Has the picture got a particular shape? Is this significant?
Look at a variety of pictures with different shapes. For example, *Christ Mocked* by Hieronymus Bosch is a very different shape from Brueghel's *Christ carrying his cross*. Bosch's picture contains five large heads: one in each corner and Christ's head in the centre. Brueghel's picture has a very tiny Christ amongst a huge crowd of people: you have to search the picture to locate him. Sometimes there are significant shapes within a picture.

In El Greco's painting of the agony in the garden, the disciples are all wrapped up within their cloaks

An adaptation of the disciples in El Greco's Agony in the garden

within a "cave" shape – were they so wrapped up in themselves that they forgot to pray?

(8) Has the picture a particular direction? Are the characters looking or moving one way? Is this significant?
Look at a picture such as *Belshazzar's feast* by Rembrandt. What is the point towards which they are looking? Why? A similar set of questions can be asked of any painting by looking at the direction of people, the focus of their eyes, or the flow of a crowd. Movement and eye focus will often draw a person's gaze to the significant action.

(9) What is happening at the centre of the picture?
Find the centres of a number of pictures with pupils. Do the artists tend to use the centre for important points? In *The resurrected Christ* by Piero della Francesca, the Risen Christ stands centrally, dividing the picture in half. The trees on one side of the picture (the side where Christ's foot is still in the grave) are barren. The trees on the other side are leafy.

(10) Where is the focal point?
Artists do not always use the centre of a picture for significant events. Each picture has its own focal point(s). How has the artist drawn your attention to it? Look through a number of pictures to find different focal points. When pupils are painting a picture of a Bible story, ask them to think carefully about where their focal point will be, and how they are going to draw people's attention to it.

(11) What is happening in the background, in the corners and edges?
Sometimes the background in which a picture is set adds to the meaning. Sometimes details tucked away in the background or on the fringes of the painting help us to understand it. Give pupils a magnifying glass to explore the details of a picture. Give pupils a Bible story. What would they tuck away in the corners to help people? What background would the picture need?

(12) Has the picture got a particular mood? How would you describe the mood?
Look at a range of pictures with the pupils, asking them to classify them according to moods. Give them a list of Bible stories. What moods would they say each story had?

(13) How has the artist created the mood of the picture?
Ask pupils what they would need to do the change the mood.

(14) How does this picture differ from others?
Sometimes what an artist doesn't do is significant. Look at the same subject painted by various artists, for example the way the baby is painted in nativity paintings. In the Portinari altarpiece by Hugo van der Goes, the baby is all alone on a stone floor, no one touches him, everyone is kneeling in worship. In one of Mantegna's "virgin and child" paintings the baby is cradled in the crook of Mary's neck: he couldn't be closer to her. The two artists reflect different aspects of the Christian belief in the two natures of Christ, his divinity and humanity.

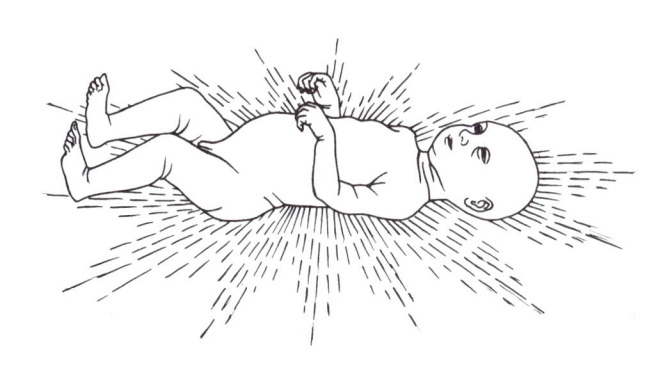

An adaption of Hugo van der Goes Christ child from the Portinari altarpiece

(15) Where is the light source? Is it focusing on anything significant?
Look at a Bible story with the pupils. If they translated this into a picture where would they place the light source? Would they use it to identify anything significant? Look at *The agony in the garden* by El Greco: here the light, in a dark painting, falls directly on Jesus.

ART

(16) What colours has the artist used? Are any colours particularly dominant?
Restrict the pupils to a certain number of colours so that their painting will have a dominant colour, or allow them to choose several colours which they think suitable for a particular story. They can then paint their own pictures experimenting with shades of those colours.

(17) Artist in a hurry
Give pupils a painting of a biblical subject and ask them to note what the artist has done in detail and what s/he has left unfocused or shadowy. In the painting *The nativity at night* ascribed to Geertgen tot Sint Jans, Joseph, the animals, and the shepherds are very shadowy; only Mary, the baby, and the angels are picked out by light. If the pupils were painting in a hurry and only had time to paint in detail a few sections, which would they choose to leave shadowy? Which would they do in detail?

(18) Is it the type of painting you could turn into drama?
Pupils might like to arrange each other in a tableau to form the painting. At a given signal, the painting comes alive. The opposite technique can be used, the pupils act out the story but freeze in the attitude of the painting when they reach that point.

(19) The photographer
Look at a variety of paintings, particularly ones with unusual angles such as Salvador Dali's *Crucifixion* (viewed from above) and Mantegna's *The dead Christ* (viewed from the feet). Ask the pupils to imagine that the painting is a photograph and they are the photographer. Where would they have to be standing to achieve the effect of the painting? Does the angle of the painting give pupils any insights into the story behind the painting?

An adaptation of The dead Christ *by Andrea Mantegna*

(20) Foreground and background
Look at a painting with reference to what is in the foreground, and what is in the background. Sometimes artists depicting the same event will put different things in the foreground. A good example of this would be the *Kitchen scene with Christ in the house of Martha and Mary* by Diego Velázquez. A very fed-up "Martha" figure dominates the foreground; Mary and Jesus are small and in the background. Select a biblical story. If you were creating a painting from this story, what would you consider important to put in the foreground? What would you leave in the background?

INTRODUCTION

Talking pictures

The twenty questions on pages 26–28 are general questions that apply to many paintings. When exploring a painting with pupils, teachers need to create questions specific to that painting. The questions should help pupils explore not only the content of the painting, but its message, the feelings of the subjects and what it might mean to Christians.

Questions should be "affective" and help the pupil relate to the work of art rather than see it as something distant or old fashioned with nothing to say to today. Below are a few examples of this type of question.

What can you read in the faces of the main characters?

Christ before the High Priest *(Caiaphas)* by Gerrit van Honthorst

What do you think they are thinking?
How would you describe the expression on …'s face?
Have you ever felt like that?
Who are the most and least important? What makes you think that?

An example

Christ before Caiaphas

What do you see?
– Lots of people, very faint. They're not the ones you should be looking at.

Who are the important people meant to be? Who's doing the talking?
– The man with the finger.

What time of day is it?
– Ten.

Where's the light coming from?
– The candle.

Who are these people?
– Guards.

Why is he [Jesus] standing up?
– He's more important.

Who do the bystanders think is more important?
– The pointing finger man.

What does this person [guard] think about it?
– People enjoying someone else's punishment.

What can you read in his [Caiaphas's] face?
– He's telling him [Jesus].
– He's warning him [Jesus].
– Evilness, threatening, unkind.

What is in the book?
– The rules.

ART

What's the finger saying?
— "If you don't do the rules I'm gonna call my guards."
— "It's about time you did what I want you to do."

What is he [Jesus] saying or thinking?
— Bored, tired, poor and sad.

What can you read in his [Jesus'] face?
— He's scared, there's no one to support him.
— Can you shut up for a minute and give me space.

Is he [Jesus] going to do what finger man says?
— He's thinking, "I'd better do what he wants me to do else he'll kill me."
— No, cos if he does what he says once, he'll have to keep on doing what he says and not what he thinks is right.

Who's got the power?
— Finger man.

What's he saying?
— "I'm the Boss."

Whose side is the painter on? Why? Where's the light?
— The guy on the right [Jesus], He's threatened, on his own, defenceless.

What kind of power has this man [Jesus] got?
— Belief in himself.
— The power to like people or hate.
— He's got the heart to make people feel good about themselves.
— Finger man is scared of his power. He's afraid he'll be the lonely one if they all do what he says.

Which of these men will you trust to tell you the truth?
— Not him [guard], he wants to kill him when no one's looking.

What kind of power has Finger man got?
— He's got guards.

Do we know who this is?
— Jesus.

Do we know the name of this person [Caiaphas]?
Silence.

Who's heard of Jesus?
— People liked him, so they put all his goodness into the Bible.
— He _told_ people and he _did_ it.
— He shows goodness and people want to believe in goodness.

Teacher and Year 3 class discussion,
Walnut Tree Walk Primary School, Kennington, London

The National Gallery provides postcards of the following. A wider range is available on transparencies.

The annunciation by Fra Filippo Lippi
The annunciation by Duccio
The adoration of the kings by Pieter Brueghel the Elder
The nativity by Piero della Francesca
Mystic nativity by Sandro Botticelli
The nativity at night ascribed to Geertgen tot Sint Jans
The adoration of the golden calf by Nicolas Poussin
The Virgin of the rocks by Leonardo da Vinci
The choir of angels by Simon Marmion
The Virgin and child in an interior by the workshop of Campin
The baptism of Christ by Piero della Francesca
The raising of Lazarus by Sebastiano del Piombo
Kitchen scene with Christ in the house of Martha and Mary by Diego Velázquez
Christ driving the traders from the Temple by El Greco
Christ mocked by Hieronymus Bosch
The agony in the garden by Andrea Mantegna
Christ before the High Priest by Gerrit van Honthorst
Head of Christ crowned with thorns after Guido Reni
The supper at Emmaus by Michelangelo Merisi da Caravaggio
Christ appearing to the Magdalene by Titian

INTRODUCTION

Thirty-three art activities

These activities are centred on biblically based art. Many of the techniques can be applied to the paintings on pages 24 and 25.

(1) Fire! Fire!
Ask the pupils to imagine there has been a fire in the art gallery. There is only time to rescue three out of the five paintings in the room devoted to biblical art. Give the pupils five pictures (use postcards). Ask them which three they would save if there was a fire. Pupils should be able to justify their choice and make a case for their painting being saved. This can be run as a balloon debate.
NOTE: the number of paintings can be varied according to the size of the class and the resources available.

(2) Close-ups
Using progressive close-ups involves pupils making three or four drawings based on a painting:

(a) a group or a person in their environment or general scene;
(b) one person on their own;
(c) one person's expression or part of their body, for example their hands.

The example of (b) given opposite is from Giotto's *Lamentation over the dead Christ*. A sheet of sugar paper can be divided into three for this. The progressive focusing can help pupils explore various characters' reactions. Look at Zacchaeus' reaction to Jesus in the pictures on page 140. Explore with the pupils what is happening.

(3) The photographer
Look at a painting and ask the pupils to compose the same scene using other pupils and objects. They can photograph the scene and compare the photograph with the original. This activity helps pupils explore the way in which composition conveys meaning. The way in which subjects are arranged is not usually accidental. Pupils can also create their own photographic compositions, based on a biblical story, using fellow pupils and objects. The photographs can then be displayed alongside the stories.

Adaption of an angel from Giotto's Lamentations over dead Christ

(4) Make a storyboard from a picture
Some pictures do not contain one event, but many. Look at the story picture on page 57, *Story and Drama* and arrange the events in the right order by putting numbers on "post-it" notes and placing them on the various parts of the picture. Give the pupils a sheet with a number of squares on it. In each square they draw a section of the picture, arranging the squares in sequence. In the first square they draw what they think is the first event and beside it they write what they think is happening. They continue until they have used all the events in the picture or painting. Pupils can check their storyboard by the biblical story on which the art is based, or they may like to read the story before attempting this exercise. See page 110, *Story and Drama*, for an example of a storyboard.
NOTE: This activity can also be done with a series of pictures such as those of Zacchaeus on page 140.

Action:

Dialogue:

Camera angle:

ART

(5) Jigsaws
Cut up a postcard of a biblical painting. Give a section, the title of the painting, and the biblical story on which it is based to each member of the group. They should write about their particular piece in detail, commenting on how they think their section of the picture relates to the story. When they have done this, they can put the picture together as a whole. Does this help in their understanding of the picture?

(6) Making drawings from written or oral descriptions
One person has a print of a painting and describes it in great detail, orally or in writing, to another, who then paints from the description. The finished work is then displayed alongside the original. This can be done from a written or oral description.

(7) Style
Look at the same image – Mary, or the resurrection, for example – across a variety of periods and styles. What are the messages of the different images?

(8) Improvising
When there are a number of characters in a painting, pupils can improvise conversations between characters. Speech bubbles can be drawn on "post-it" notes and placed on pictures.

(9) Creating the picture
Recreate the picture using pupils, costumes, and props. Others can then paint from a photograph of this recreated version. It can be combined with questions which will help probe meaning. For example, why do you think the artist arranged them in that way?

(10) Borrowing
Pupils can "borrow" from an artist's work, making their own copy of a painting or using a particular artist's technique. This helps them add that particular technique to their own repertoire and analyse how effects are created. Again, this helps them to focus on, rather than glance over, a painting. Learning from other artists gives them greater freedom in their own expression, as it adds to their range of techniques with which to express their own ideas.

(11) Across cultures
Use paintings of the same story or image but from various cultures. Examine the ways in which various cultures express the same image – for example Jesus in various cultures. (A poster set called "Jesus worldwide" is available from the Christian Education Movement (CEM).)

(12) Eyes
After they have looked at a painting, ask pupils to focus on just the eyes or the hands. What do they express? Hands or eyes across a number of paintings can be explored. For example look at the hands and the mouths of the three shepherds in the Portinari altarpiece by Hugo van der Goes. Look at the hands in the Zacchaeus pictures on page 140.

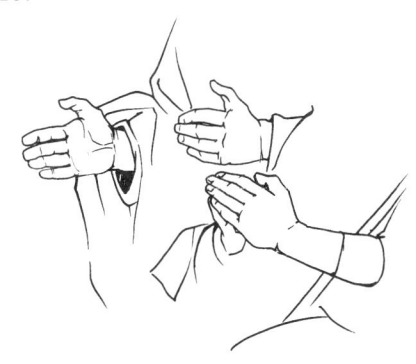

An adaption of the hands of the shepherds from the Portinari altarpiece.

(13) "I like" and "I hate"
Give the pupils a selection of biblical works and ask them to pick out two they like and two they do not like. Ask them to give a set number of reasons for liking or disliking each picture.

(14) Clothes
Look at a biblical picture. Ask pupils if they can tell anything about the characters from their clothes. Look at Zacchaeus in comparison with the rest of the crowd (page 140).

(15) Letter writing
Give pupils a print of a painting and ask them to write a letter to the artist asking him or her about their art or about the meaning of a particular painting. What questions would they want to ask?

INTRODUCTION

(16) Different forms
Give pupils the same subject expressed in different art forms – sculpture, woodcarving, book illustration, tapestry, stained glass and so on. Which do they like and why? Which form do they feel is most expressive of the significance of the event?

(17) Restoration
Give the pupils a postcard or a reproduction of a picture. Explain that the picture has been badly damaged. If they could afford to restore only part of the picture, which part would they choose? Which part do they think is significant?

(18) Symbols
Explore the use of symbols and the symbolic use of colour with the pupils. Look at pictures dating from the Middle Ages. Use the symbol dictionary on page 67 and the colour code to "read" the pictures. Give the pupils the symbolic colours chart. How many can they find in the picture of the annunciation on page 141?

An adaption of the dove from Rosetti's Annunciation

(19) Placing poems and prose next to pictures
Display poems and pictures alongside each other. Pupils should be given the poem but have a choice of pictures on that subject from which they can choose. For example:

"O Simplicitas" by Madeleine L'Engle (*Oxford Book of Christmas Poems* edited by M Harrison and C Stuart Clark (OUP, 1983)) and Rossetti's painting *The annunciation*. (Secondary)

"Heaven" by L Hughs (*Whispering in God's Ear* compiled by A MacDonald (Lion, 1994)) and *The peaceable Kingdom* by E Hicks. (Primary)

(20) Images
Select one image from a picture and write about it: a gawking shepherd or a smiling angel. This can be done as a random exercise. Ask pupils to list all the characters which appear in a picture. Place the names in a hat and pull them out at random.

(21) Brainstorm
Using large sheets of paper, brainstorm all the emotions and reactions which occur in a picture. These can be classified into positive and negative reactions, which can then be explored.

(22) Body Sculpture
Sculpt a person into the position a character holds in a painting, for example *Job* by James Daugherty. By feeling the position the artist has drawn, they may be able to explore what he was saying by that particular piece of body language. Sculpting can be done verbally, without touch.

An adaption of Job *by James Daugherty*

ART

(23) Make a viewfinder
Cut a small rectangular hole in a large piece of card. Place this over a picture so that pupils concentrate on one part only, blotting out the rest. What does this part of the picture say on its own without its context? Can the pupils guess the rest of the picture?

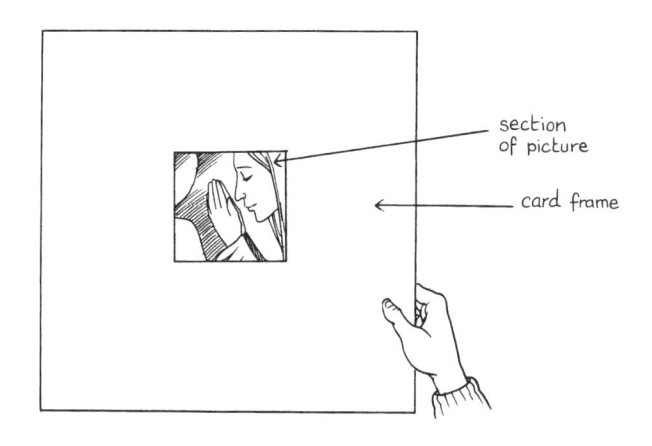

(24) Role play
Pupils can role play certain characters in the picture. A few props may help them get into role. Other pupils can then question them. Pupils can read the biblical story which lies behind the picture to get into role. For notes on role play see pages 83–86 *Story and Drama*.

(25) Using local artists
Invite into school local Christians who use art to express their faith. Ask the pupils to devise a set of questions they could ask.

(26) Questions
Ask the pupils to write three questions about a work of art, based on the painting and the story it portrays. The finished questions can be given to another group to answer.

A factual question about content (Where does the action take place? etc.).
A question relating to significance and interpretation (Why do you think...?).
A question involving a personal response (Do you think the artist was right to...?).

(27) Music
Ask pupils to select pieces of music to go with certain works of art which will reflect the mood and meaning.

(28) Research the life of a particular painter
Did personal experience affect how he or she drew?

(29) Explore biblical art in use
Most religious art is not created to be placed in galleries and museums. It is living art with a purpose. Explore the art in local churches and how it is used as part of worship.

(30) Guide books
Write an entry for a guidebook on a picture, indicating significant points. This can be part of a "biblical gallery" created in a corner of the classroom.

(31) Falling in
Pupils can explore the idea of what it would be like to become part of a picture. Choose a picture with plenty of characters. If they were to become part of the picture, which person would they want to be? Why? Would they want to be an onlooker instead? Where would they stand? What would they see from their perspective? (Avoid pictures of the crucifixion or similar pictures for this exercise.)

(32) First impressions, last impressions
Show a painting to the pupils and ask for first impressions. Leave it hanging for at least a week, longer if you see pupils infrequently. See if their opinion changes after a period of time.

(33) Art swap
Pupils should be allowed to browse through biblical art books, postcards of biblical art, old Christmas cards, etc., and select a favourite. This can be shared with others and reasons given for why they like it.

DETAILED ACTIVITIES

Banners

Creation: Psalm 8
The "I Am" sayings: John 6.35; 8.12; 9.5; 10.9, 11; 11.25, 26; 14.6; 15.1–5
The call of the disciples: Matthew 4.18–22; Mark 1.14–20

Description of the activity

Banners are popular in many churches and are used to express a variety of stories and beliefs. Before pupils attempt to make their own, they should look at a number of banners to explore how they are made, and the means used to express ideas. Texture, size, proportion, shape, and colour should be noted. If possible, visit a local church which uses banners, or alternatively a member of a banner-making group may be able to visit the school and explain what they do.

Banners can be made from fabric which can be sewn or glued on using a safe fabric glue. Banners can also be made from paper, and different textures and types of paper applied. Paper banners are a quick method for the classroom. If it is not practical to make finished banners in the classroom, designs for banners can be created on the computer or by hand.

Examples

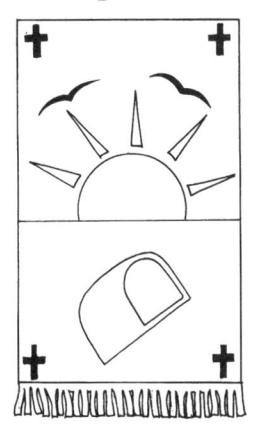

Banners by pupils of Binscombe Middle School, Godalming

ART

Biblical application

Banners can be used to express beliefs, characters, and stories. They can express a belief, such as God the creator (Psalm 8), depict a person, such as Jesus as the good shepherd, or illustrate a story or piece of text, such as "Follow me" (the calling of the disciples).

After studying the way in which banners are made, pupils can make their own banners to illustrate a story or character, or to express a belief. Pupils should begin by studying the story or text involved and discussing its meaning. A set of banners can be made for the "I am" sayings, each one expressing a different saying. The stories and sayings can be shared out among groups within a class.

Calligrams

Love: 1 Corinthians 13.1–13
Anger: Ephesians 4.26
Fear: Psalm 46.1–2
Worry: Matthew 6.25; Proverbs 12.25
Envy and jealousy: Proverbs 27.4; Song of Songs 8.6–7
Pride: Proverbs 16.18
Evil speech: Proverbs 12.18
Wealth: Ecclesiastes 5.10
Peace: Proverbs 14.30
Kind words: Proverbs 15.4

Description of the activity

Calligrams are words drawn in a way that expresses their meaning. They can be created on the computer using a draw or paint package, or can be created using paint, collage, rubbings, etc.

Not only the shapes of letters, but also the colour, texture and medium used can help express meaning. The word SOFT could be made from padded fabric; the word ROUGH from very coarse material; the word FIRE from red foil.

An example
Evil speech

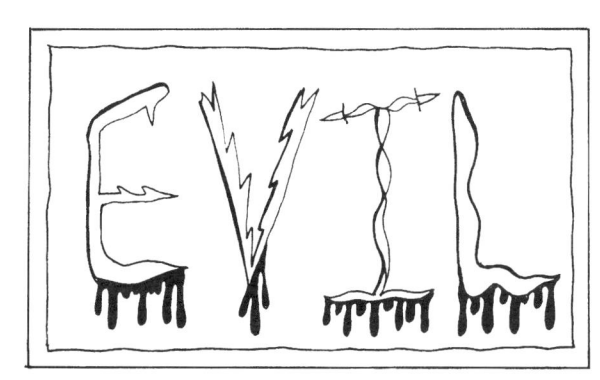

Bytom Green, Year 7, Brambletye Middle School, Surrey

DETAILED ACTIVITIES

Biblical application

Pupils can look at various subjects such as joy, peace, and hatred, and research biblical teaching on these subjects. The words can be written as calligrams to express their essential character and any insights the pupils gained from the biblical material. Biblical material can also be written underneath. In each case, the essential character of the word should be discussed.

Stained glass

Christmas: Matthew 1.18—2.18; Luke 1.26–38; 2.1–20
Easter: Matthew 27.32–50
Pentecost: Acts 2.1–13
Harvest: Deuteronomy 17.9–17

Description of the activity

Stained glass is one form of Christian art which is usually available in some form in the local community. Pupils should look at a variety of stained glass, modern and ancient, and make sketches or take photographs so that they are aware of the range of the art form. If possible they should see pictures of stained glass by famous artists such as Burne-Jones, Piper and Chagall. Some basic books on stained glass are listed on page 22.

There are various ways of making stained-glass windows with pupils. Here are two examples.

(1) Make the basic window shape from black card or sugar paper. Paste tracing paper over the back. Pencil onto the paper the basic design and decide on the colours. Draw on the lines which will represent the black lead. Using a clear glue and coloured tissue paper fill in the appropriate sections by pasting tissue paper to the tracing paper. Alternatively, fill in the coloured sections with wax crayons or large, safe, felt-tip pens. Using a black wax crayon or a large felt tip, fill in the black "lead" lines.

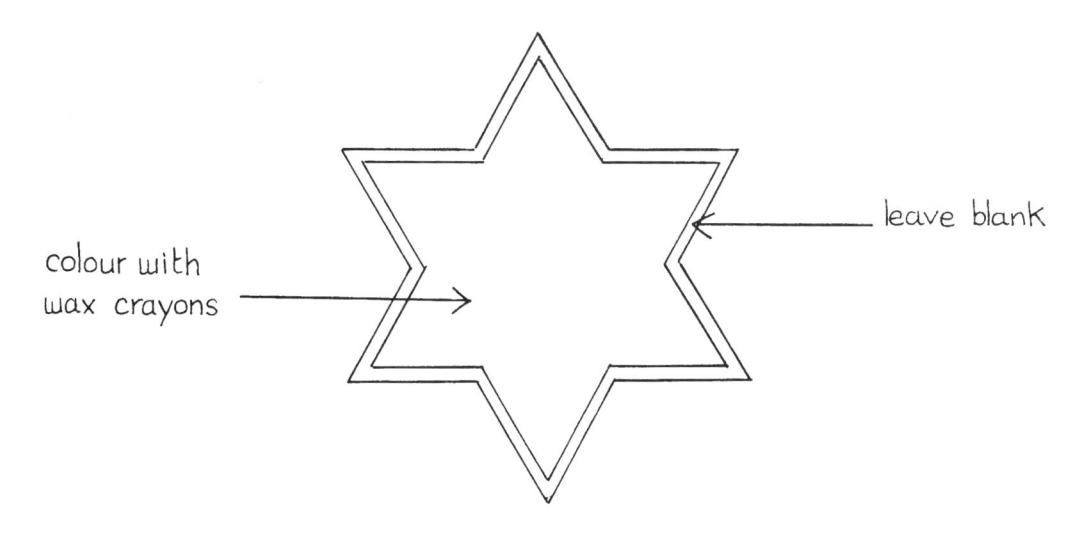

(2) Stained-glass windows can also be painted. Draw the basic window on white paper. Lightly pencil in the design, leaving a space for the black lead lines. Colour in the main design and background using either oil pastels or wax crayon (thickly). When finished, paint over the whole window with diluted black paint.

Biblical application
Stained glass can be used for biblical symbols, or for scenes and people. The drawings need to be kept simple. In the case of the festivals, there are many symbols which can be used (see pages 67–70). The windows can be abstract in design. Many modern stained-glass windows in cathedrals such as Coventry, Derby, and Liverpool use colour and shape to express meaning. Before any design is attempted, pupils should be able to see how Christians have expressed their faith in this art form, and have time to discuss the story they want to communicate in this way.

Marbling

Creation: Genesis 1.1—2.25
Elijah's fiery chariot: 2 Kings 2.1–18
Jonah: The Book of Jonah
Paul's shipwreck: Acts 27.1–10

Description of the activity
Special, safe, marbling inks are carefully floated on a tray of water. The floating patterns can be gently stirred to give the pattern movement, or combed with a wide toothed comb. Absorbent paper such as newsprint is lowered into the water and lifted off again. It is important not to get bubbles of air trapped underneath. The paper absorbs the pattern which captures the movement of the inks on water.

Further prints can be taken using the remains of the ink still floating in the water. This will give very pale delicate patterns.

As marbling captures movement, it is very good for subjects such as water and flames. The prints can be cut or torn and used in different ways.

A cheap way of doing a form of marbling is to use ordinary liquid paint on a perspex or formica surface. Swirl or comb the colours together and then print as if doing a monoprint (page 61).

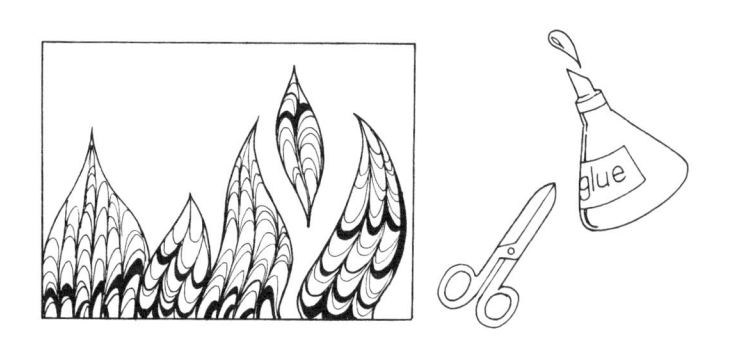

DETAILED ACTIVITIES

Biblical application

After reading a story, pupils should discuss its meaning and the emotions experienced by the characters. They then discuss how they could use marbling to express that meaning. For example, what colours would express a particular emotion? Would the colour need to be deep and vivid or pale and watery to communicate that feeling?

A collage of the story of Jonah can be created using marbled paper for the sky and water, and plain coloured paper for the figures, the fish, and the ship, to give contrast. Using deep colours for the marbling with lots of movement can help children depict the wildness of the storm and the desperation of the sailors in the story of Paul. The flames of Elijah's chariot can be created from marbled paper. The fiery chariot is a symbol of God coming to "carry Elijah home" in the words of the spiritual. The flames can be awesome, but there is also a message about a close relationship in the story which can be explored with the pupils. Awe is not terror.

The variety of creation can be expressed through marbling which is cut and used as collage (page 40). The emphasis should be on variety and beauty.

Using a church

The Ten Commandments: Deuteronomy 5.1–21
The good shepherd: John 10.1–21

Description of the activity

This activity involves using a church as both stimulation and subject matter for RE and art. In the Middle Ages, the church was called "the Bible of the poor". In an age when were people could not read, a variety of visual forms were used. During a visit to a suitable church, pupils can list as many different art forms as possible: statues, symbols, stained glass, architecture, carving, embroidery, painting, and so forth. These can become the subject of the pupils' own rubbings, drawings, paintings and clay work.

Biblical application

The subject matter of much of the art in churches is biblical. Teachers would need to make a preliminary visit and have available the stories on which some of the art is based. As many pupils will not know which have a biblical basis and which do not, it is helpful if the teacher has the biblical references around the church on pieces of card, placed by the relevant pieces of art so that pupils can explore how a piece of art relates to a story.

ART

Biblical stories such as Christ the good shepherd may be found in windows or plaster, in paintings or wood carvings. There may be statues of biblical figures. Many of the symbols which appear in sacred art have a biblical root (see pages 67–70). The Ten Commandments may be on the wall or verses of Scripture painted on the plaster. Having seen the many ways in which the church uses art to express the meaning of a story, the pupils can read a Bible story and choose one of the methods they have seen to express it themselves, or write why they would choose that particular medium.

Collage

The fiery furnace: Daniel 3.1–30
The plumbline: Amos 7.7–9
The transfiguration: Matthew 17.1–13; Mark 9.2–13; Luke 9.28–36
The ascension: Mark 16.19–20; Luke 24.50–53; Acts 1.1–11

Description of the activity

Collage can be created from a variety of materials such as fabric, paper, tissue, foil, rubbings, marbled paper, newspaper, wallpapers, or magazines. Attention should be given to colour, texture, the overall shape, and the mood created.

Biblical application

The variety of textures and colours used in collage creates mood and can be used to interpret the biblical story or passage. The decision-making involved in selecting images, colours, and so on gives the pupils a context in which to discuss the story and its meaning.

The fiery furnace can be made from foils and cellophanes and suitable colours cut from magazines. Pupils should listen to the story and decide how they could create a fire effect. The emphasis should be on the danger the three men were prepared to enter.

The image of the plumbline is one of judgement. In Coventry Cathedral, there stands a sculpture of this image – a plumbline suspended over a modern city. (See illustration on page 142.) The message is clear: "What would God judge modern society for?" Pupils might like to create their own collage of the plumbline, including what they would judge to be wrong in society.

The transfiguration and ascension involve light, which can be expressed through collage. In the transfiguration, the disciples suddenly see Jesus differently. They see the other side of him, Jesus the Son of God rather than the Son of Man. A rubbing of Jesus can be made by placing a cardboard figure under the paper and rubbing with a crayon, the surrounding "light" being created from collage. The same can be done for the ascension. Clouds which hide Jesus from the disciples' sight can be surrounded with light. A shining cloud, light, and fire are all symbols of the presence of God in the Bible.

DETAILED ACTIVITIES

Rubbings

Noah: Genesis 6.1—9.17
The temptation: Matthew 4.1–11; Mark 1.12–13; Luke 4.1–13
The garden of Gethsemane: Matthew 26.36–46; Mark 14.32–42; Luke 22.39–46; John 18.1–11
Elijah on Mount Carmel: 1 Kings 18.16–46

Description of the activity

A variety of surfaces can be used to create rubbings – embossed papers, concrete, wood, stone, etc. Rubbings can be made with pencils, crayon and pastels as well as with specially designed sticks. The resulting rubbings can be cut to create a collage. Rubbings can also be made by cutting shapes or figures from card and placing these under paper and rubbing. This results in a very shadowy picture. The cardboard shapes can be moved about under the paper to create a crowd, waves, clouds, and so on.

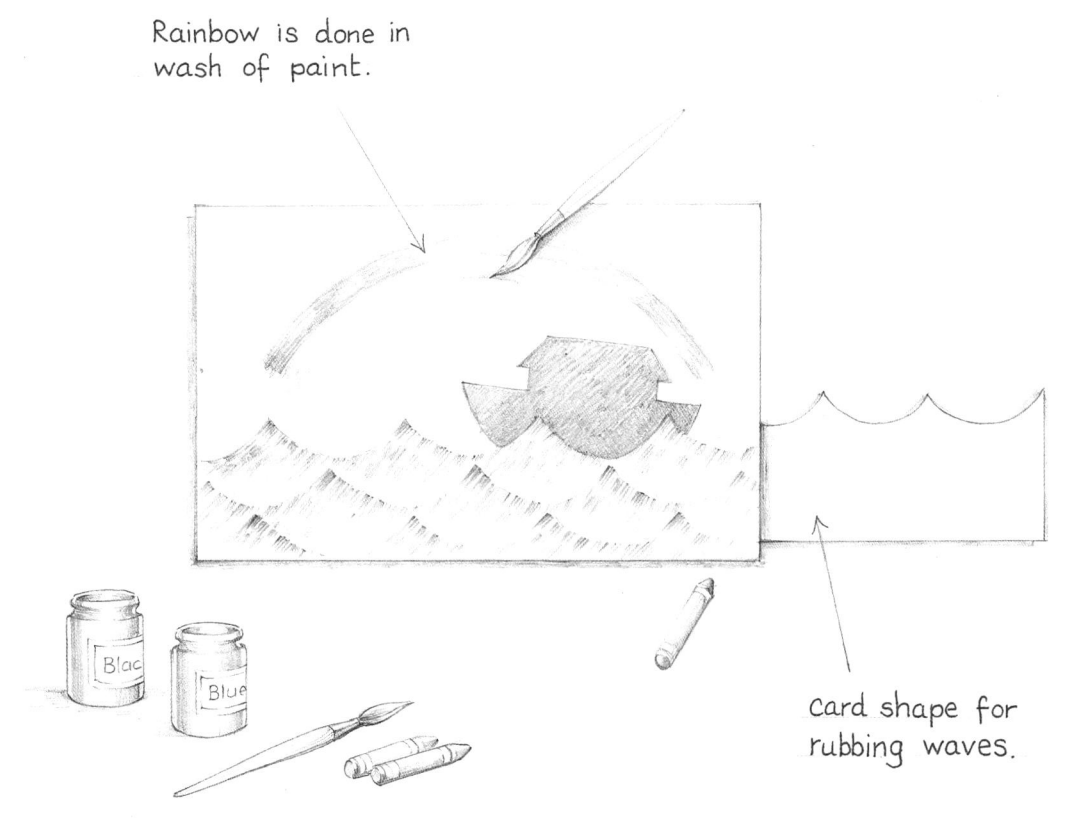

Rainbow is done in wash of paint.

card shape for rubbing waves.

Biblical application

Rubbings can be used to create scenes. Cut card in wave shapes and keep rubbing and moving them under a large sheet of paper to create a sea scene. A basic ark shape can then be added. Rocks and hills can be created in suitable colours from rubbings, to create a background for the story of the temptation.

Rubbings can make shadowy pictures all in grey, or in one colour to which just a hint of colour could be added using another technique (such as water wash). Noah's ark and the sea can be done in black wax crayon or pencil, and a rainbow added in water wash (page 45). This gives the bleakness and despair of the flood but the promise of hope.

A figure can be placed under paper and continually moved and rubbed to create a crowd for the scene on Mount Carmel, emphasizing Elijah's lone stand against the majority. Shadowy rubbings of trees and hills cut from card can be used to form a dark garden scene for Jesus in Gethsemane. Crosses can be rubbed to create a crucifixion scene, and a symbol of hope can be added such as a coloured "dawn" background. The emphasis should be on creating the mood of the story and picking out significant details in colour. The mood, meaning, and significance of a story should be discussed with pupils before they start their rubbings.

Stolen picture

The annunciation: Luke 1.26–38; and *The annunciation* by Dante Gabriel Rossetti, page 141.
The writing on the wall: Daniel 5.1–31; and *Belshazzar's feast* by Rembrandt van Rijn, page 139.

Description of the activity

Give the pupils a picture frame photocopied onto a piece of paper. Have a print of a painting (on a biblical subject) hidden: do not show the pupils the print but have the title of the painting written on the photocopied picture frame.

Ask younger pupils to imagine that thieves have broken into the art gallery and stolen the painting. With older pupils just give them the photocopied sheet with the title of the painting and the biblical reference for the story. Ask the pupils to read the story and discuss in pairs how the artist may have expressed it.

Who would be in the picture?
What would their expressions be?
How would the relationship between the people be expressed (eye-contact, grouping, etc.)?
What symbols might be used? (See pages 67–70.)
What colours would be used? (See page 67.)

Other questions can be found on pages 29–30.

When pupils have finished this, ask them to produce either their own version of what the painting may have looked like, either as a rough sketch or as a painting, or a diagram and notes to explain what it may have looked like. Show the pupils the print of the painting and discuss their interpretation of the story and the artist's. Display the finished results alongside the print at the end of the activity.

DETAILED ACTIVITIES

Diagram and notes

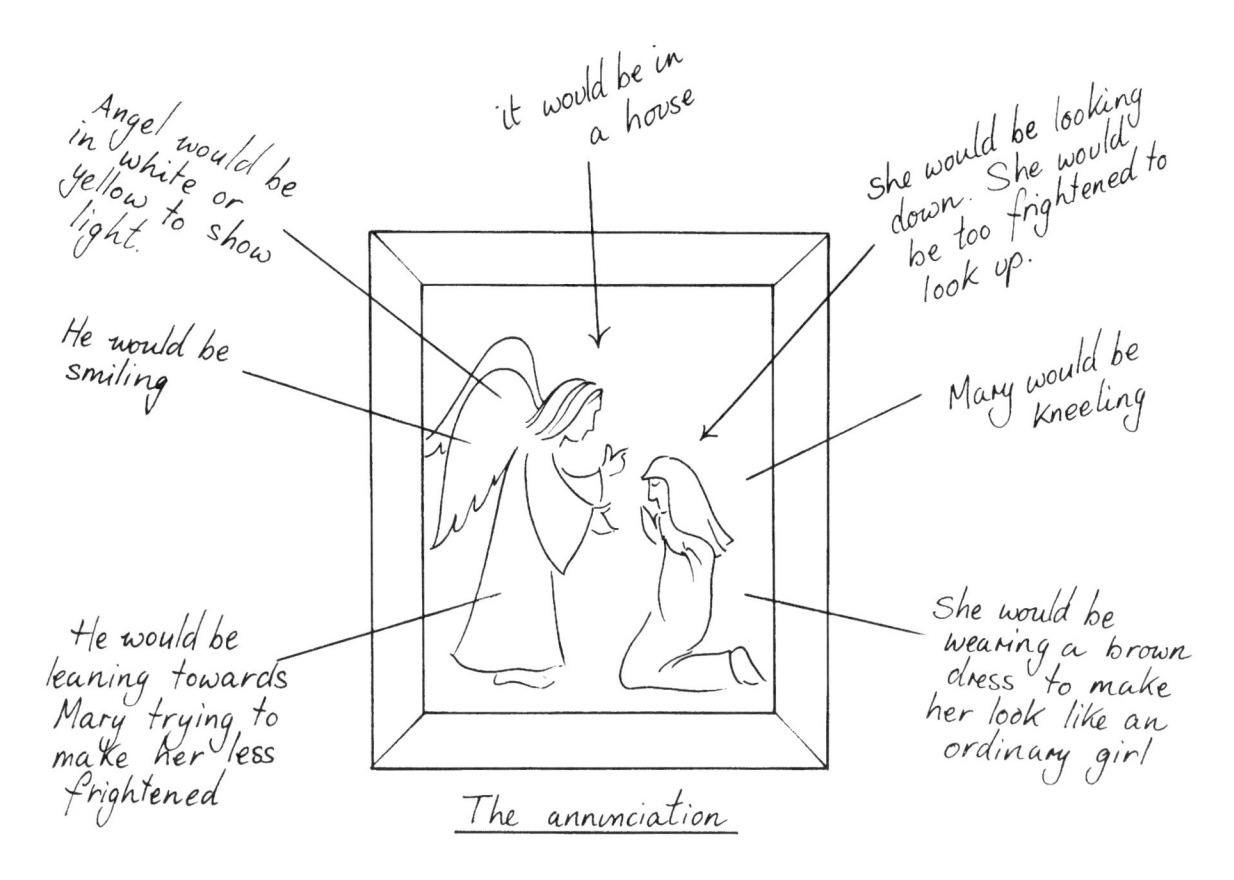

Diagram of "The annunciation" with handwritten annotations:
- Angel would be in white or yellow to show light.
- He would be smiling
- He would be leaning towards Mary trying to make her less frightened
- it would be in a house
- she would be looking down. She would be too frightened to look up.
- Mary would be kneeling
- She would be wearing a brown dress to make her look like an ordinary girl

An example
Virgin and Child by Andrea Mantegna

In my picture Mary is standing, she is holding the baby close, she is happy, the baby has just been born. Mary is laughing, she has had the baby, it's over, no more worry.

Laura Marinelli, Year 3, Albany Junior School, Stapleford

Biblical application

If this activity is done in an RE lesson rather than an art lesson, a picture frame can be photocopied onto a small A4 or A5 sheet. Pupils can then draw what they think the painting looked like and what the artist would have been trying to express through the painting. If pupils do not have time to do the drawing in detail, they can indicate the composition in writing with a few rough sketches or pin people and notes on how they would be grouped, dressed, and so forth, and why. It is important that pupils have some time to discuss the significance and meaning of the story before they start drawing or writing.

ART

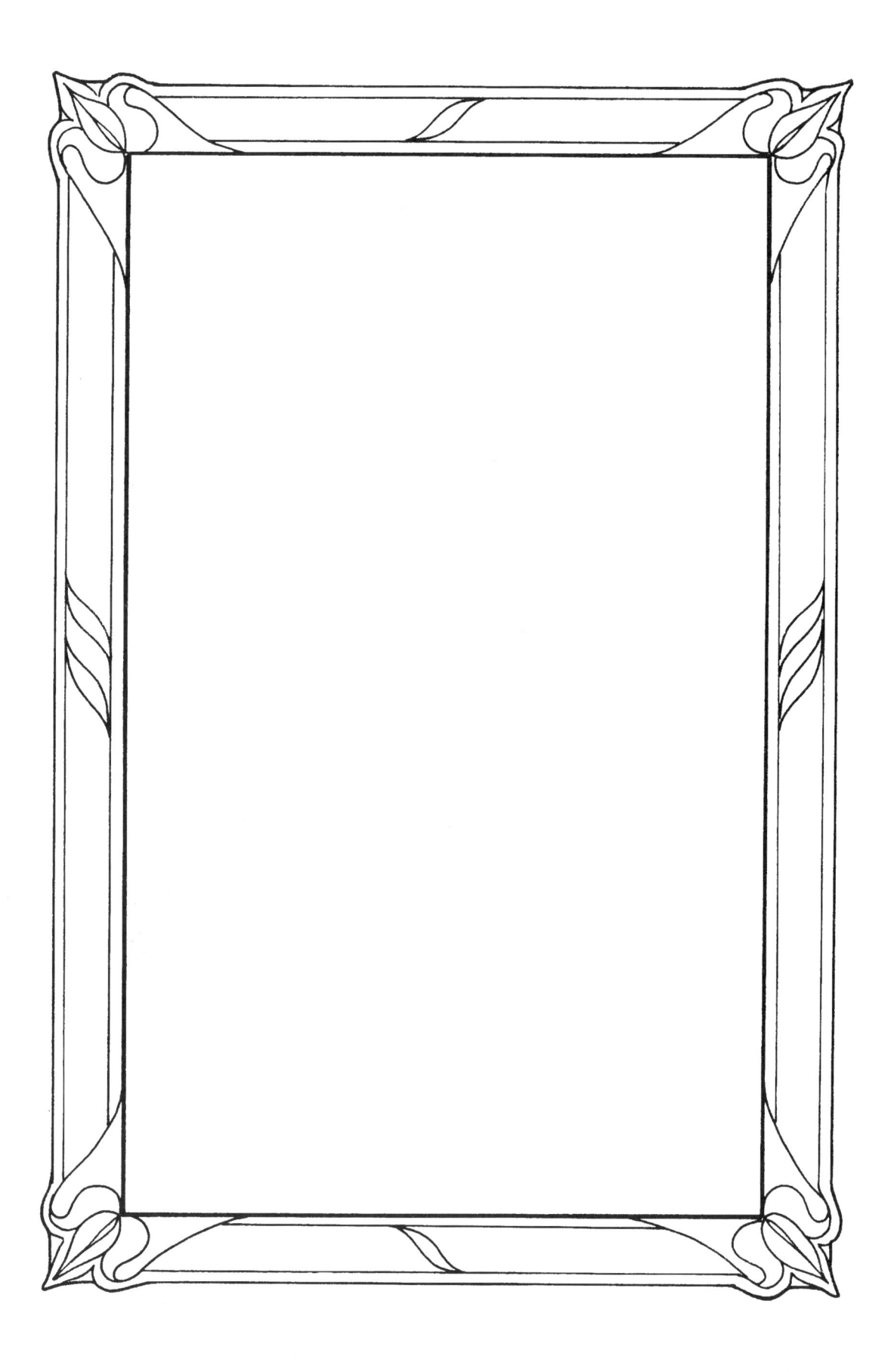

© 1996 Bible Society. This page may be photocopied for classroom use only.

Water wash

The giving of the Ten Commandments: Exodus 19.1—20.21
Jesus walks on water: Matthew 14.22–36; Mark 6.45–56; John 6.16–24
The conversion of Saint Paul: Acts 9.1–19

Description of the activity

Water wash is a quick and easy way of creating background which can be quite "atmospheric". Damp paper can be painted in streaks with water colours or diluted powder paint, and the bands of colour allowed to merge. The same can be done with slightly thicker colours on slightly damp paper which is then lightly sprayed with a "mister". Remind the pupils that the paintings always dry considerably lighter in colour. Paint can be applied with a sponge or a rag as well as a brush.

Colour is painted in bands and allowed to merge.

Biblical application

The atmosphere created by a background can help communicate meaning. A silhouette of a cross against an angry sky created with water wash will say more than a cross on its own. Pupils should start by reading a biblical story and discussing its meaning. They should write down a number of words that they think sum up its "mood", and decide which range of colours reflects that mood. A rough drawing can be created on the computer, and the menu used to keep changing the background colour until the pupils feel they have the colour they need. For example, in the story of Saint Paul, a water wash of yellows can act as a background to a painting or silhouette of the Damascus road experience. A wash of purples and reds can create a background to the scene on Mount Sinai.

ART

Computer design

Selections from Jesus' teaching
An eye for an eye: Matthew 5.38–42
The camel through the eye of the needle: Luke 18.18–30
Salt and light: Matthew 5.13–16

Description of the activity

The paint and draw packages which come with many computers can be used creatively and as an aid to learning in RE. They can aid children's drawing and design – mistakes are easy to delete and designs can be rotated, repeated, enlarged and shrunk. A computer program is, however, a tool, not an end in itself. Pupils can experiment with the way colour can affect the mood of a picture by creating a landscape or background to a picture, then use the menu to change the colour, finally selecting the colour they think best reflects the mood and meaning of the story.

The computer offers a range of tools (spray, wash, draw, etc.), which can be used in a similar way to their traditional counterparts, but the effects are different. The cut and paste facility allows images to be moved and positioned. The computer gives the pupil flexibility: nothing is final until they decide it is finished. Images can always be erased, changed or moved.

Pupils can benefit from the best of both worlds by creating drawings using traditional media, tracing them onto an acetate, which is then Blu-tacked over the computer screen. The computer draw program can be used to recreate the picture. The computer version and the traditional version can be compared. This technique is helpful for pupils who find a felt pen or pencil easier than a mouse. It then allows the pupils to experiment with their basic drawing, using the facilities of the computer.

In practice, many schools do not have the facilities for colour printing so much of the work will have to be done in black and white.

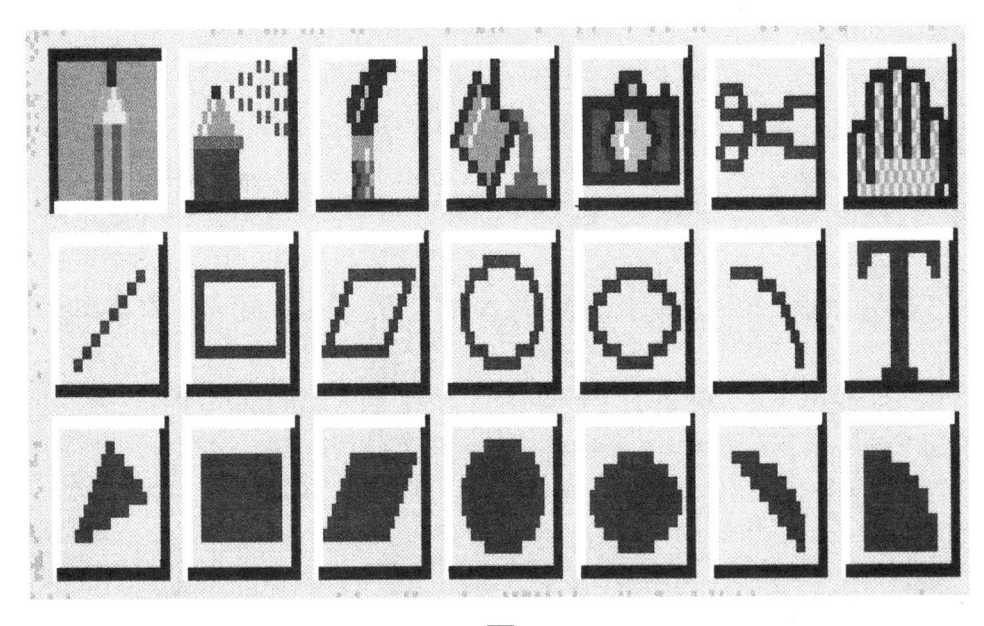

DETAILED ACTIVITIES

Biblical application

Background for biblical pictures can be created, with the emphasis on expressing the mood or feeling of the event. Whole pictures can be generated, using the computer, which express the meaning of biblical teaching such as "an eye for an eye" or "let your light shine". The emphasis should be on getting beneath the story to its meaning by using the various tools.

The year 2000 could be seen as the bi-millennium of Christianity. Pupils can generate a stamp design to commemorate this event. To do this, they will need to know some of the important people and events associated with Christianity – the birth of Jesus, his death and resurrection, the coming of the Holy Spirit, and the ongoing family of Christians, the Church. Four stamps (of four different denominations) could be produced using computer designs.

Rainbow

Computer version by Claire Balderson and Angela Saccomando, George Spencer School, Stapleford

Original rainbow stamp by Leon Tanner, Year 3, Rainey Endowed School, Magherafelt

ART

Dove stamp
Philip Michael, Year 3, Rainey Endowed School, Magherafelt

Computer design by Claire Balderson and Angela Saccomando, George Spencer School, Stapleford

DETAILED ACTIVITIES

Book jackets

The plagues of Egypt: Exodus 7.14—11.10
The life of Jeremiah: Jeremiah 1.1–19; 19.1–5; 38.1–28
The ten lepers: Luke 17.11–19
The lost sheep: Luke 15.1–7

Description of the activity
For this activity, pupils need to look at a number of book jackets and try to guess the contents of the book. Pupils can bring in books to create a book display of favourite cover designs. Types of design can be classified: cartoon, photographic, lettering, etc. Pupils need to assess how successful the artist has been in capturing the content and meaning of the story by their cover design. Pupils can then design their own jacket for a given story.

An example
Book cover design for the story of the fiery furnace

Sophie Warren, Year 6, Brambletye Middle School, Redhill

Biblical application
Show the pupils a number of book covers for stories from the Bible such as those in the reference box, for these are often published as separate stories. After reading a Bible story and discussing its meaning, pupils can design their own cover to communicate that story and message. With the story of Jeremiah, they might use some of the images such as a broken pot or a scroll, but they might also explore the idea of a message ignored.

Once pupils have decided upon their design and executed it, they can explain why they have created that particular design and how it would help the reader to understand what the book is about.

ART

Mosaic

Jonah: The Book of Jonah
Fishers of men: Mark 1.14–20; Luke 5.1–11
The feeding of the five thousand: John 6.1–15

Description of the activity

Paper mosaic can be used in place of the ceramic originals. Pupils should start by collecting piles of different shades and colours cut from magazines or plain coloured paper. These can be cut into strips of a uniform width by the teacher with a guillotine. Pupils can then chop them into squares with scissors (do not make them too small). The colours should be sorted into boxes so that it is easy for pupils to choose the right colours when they start designing.

Larger mosaics (the size of a large sheet of sugar paper) are big enough for a group to work on. Outlines should be drawn first and these outlines filled in with dark coloured squares before other colours are selected to fill in the rest of the picture. The squares which are used to fill in can follow the shape of the outline rather than filling in a uniform manner. This gives mosaic its flowing patterns. Simple shapes should be used: symbols are ideal.

An apple, a symbol of salvation

Biblical application

Mosaic was an art practised by the Christians of the Roman empire, and we still have beautiful mosaics of biblical stories. The medium is suitable for symbols when making small pictures, but it can be used for landscapes and figures for large pictures such as Jonah, and the feeding of the five thousand. If using Christian symbols information can be found on pages 67–70. Select a symbol to explore, and give the pupils a story which relates to it – for the fish symbol, this could be the call of the disciples. The symbol can be expressed in mosaic by the pupils in a way that helps people understand the story. For example, in the story of Jonah the size of the waves and the size of the fish in proportion to Jonah
can say something about the apparent hopelessness of the situation.

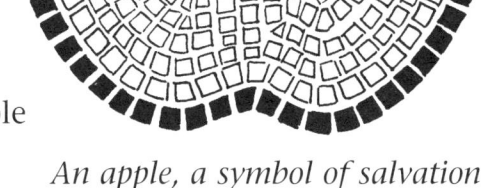

Calligraphy

Do not worry: Luke 12.22–34; Matthew 6.25–34
God the good shepherd: Psalm 23
Praise the Lord: Psalm 150
Wise behaviour: Psalm 1.1–4

Description of the activity

Calligraphy is the art of writing. There are many different scripts available and pupils can explore these initially through the fonts in a computer program, and then try lettering themselves. Time should be taken in planning and drawing faintly in pencil to produce even lettering for the main text and the outline of a large initial letter. This is easily done by using fine blue-lined graph paper. When the lettering and the outline of the large initial letter is complete, the graph paper can be photocopied, as the lines of the graph paper are not picked up by the photocopier but the black writing is. The photocopy can then be illuminated.

An example
Capital W from the word "wealth" (Ecclesiastes 5.10)

David McCubbine, Year 7, Brambletye Middle School, Redhill

Biblical application

Christians have practised calligraphy and illumination for over a thousand years. Postcards and facsimiles of The Lindisfarne Gospels and of Armenian and Ethiopian manuscripts are available from the British Museum. Postcards and facsimiles of The Book of Kells are available from The Book Shop, Trinity College, Dublin 2. The company "Bellerophon" market many colouring books which show medieval lettering and illustration. These can be cut up and mounted as examples. They do not have to be used as colouring books. The relevant titles and the address are given on page 22.

ART

Calligraphy can be used to express the meaning of various texts or stories from the Bible. The Psalms are particularly suitable, as individual verses can be used. Decorated initial letters can be filled with symbols, drawings, and colours which reflect the meaning of a biblical passage. It is essential that time is given to discussing the meaning of the story or text so that pupils can create suitable drawings to fit inside their initial letter. Symbols can be found on pages 67–70.

Visual images

Trouble like a flood: Psalm 69.1–4, 14.21
God the fortress: Psalm 18.1–5
The Lord is king: Psalm 97.1–6
Praise the Lord: Psalm 150

Description of the activity
This technique involves listening to a psalm and noting down, on scrap paper, the images which occur. A whole piece of paper (any size) is taken to represent the psalm, and within that the pupils can draw, paint, print, or stick on the visual forms of the verbal images. The idea is to fill the whole paper with images, if possible with no gaps.

Biblical application
There are many psalms in the Bible which would be suitable. Pupils should discuss the meaning of the images within a psalm before they start trying to capture the meaning of that image by their choice of colour or texture. For example, if the psalmist likens sorrow to a sea in which he is drowning, pupils might want to fill part of the paper with a seascape using thick paint which can be combed to create the effect of movement.

DETAILED ACTIVITIES

Wax resist

The woman of Shunem's son: 2 Kings 4.8–37
The raising of Lazarus: John 11.1–44
Jairus's daughter: Matthew 9.18–26; Mark 5.21–43; Luke 8.40–56
Dorcas: Acts 9.32–43

Description of the activity

This technique involves the children drawing with wax crayons and then painting over the picture with diluted paint. For a while, the picture disappears and then it comes through. Surplus paint can be blotted off the picture with blotting paper or kitchen towel. For a slightly more delicate effect, try using food dye mixed with water to paint over the picture. Oil pastels can also be used, and inks can be substituted for paint.

Biblical application

This technique can be used on many subjects. It can be used to create whole pictures. It can be used to create stained-glass windows (page 37).

The technique itself also acts as a parable when using it on the resurrection (Matthew 28.1–7) or any of the stories of life out of death (Lazarus, Jairus's daughters, etc.). Just as the picture is momentarily blotted out by the paint, but eventually comes through, so the disciples' hope was blotted out when Jesus died, only to be restored at the resurrection. A simple picture can be used for this activity; it could be a smiling face or a "rising sun", or a similar symbol, which is temporarily blotted out by the paint.

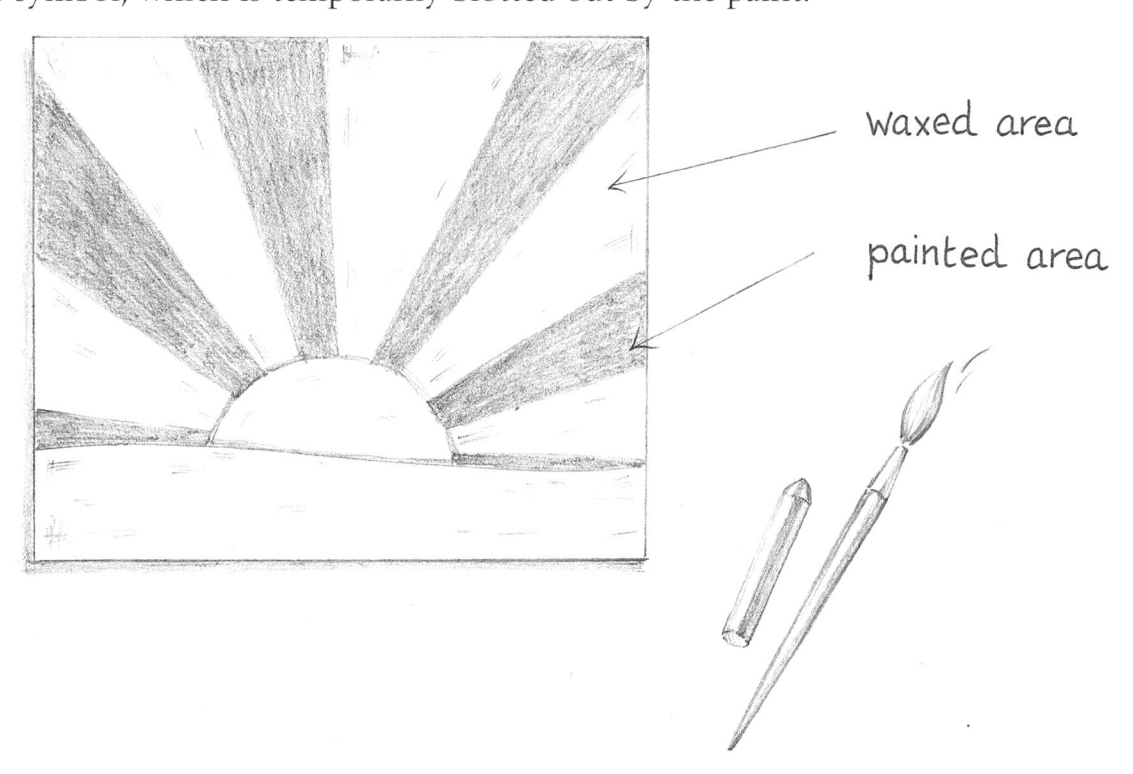

ART

Wool wrapping

Joseph: Genesis 37.39–45
Ruth: The Book of Ruth
David – king, musician, warrior: 1 Samuel 16.1–13; 17.1–58; 2 Samuel 5.1–5; 16.14–23
The lame man at the gate: Acts 3.1–10

Description of the activity

Wool can be wound round strips of card, the colours being chosen to reflect moods and events. Cut a strip of card about 2 cm wide and 10 cm long. The card used to back pads of writing paper or cereal packets is suitable. Place a strip of double-sided tape along its length (both sides). Give pupils a wide variety of thick coloured wools. The pupils, after reading a story, decide what colours would reflect the meaning of that story. For example, one group of pupils chose black, greys and maroons to reflect Good Friday. Others chose purples and browns.

A strip of wool winding can also represent a person's life. Pupils research a character, writing down the main events in their life and how they would describe those events: exciting, sad, dull, and so on. They then select colours (in wool) which they think express those events, and wind them along the strip.

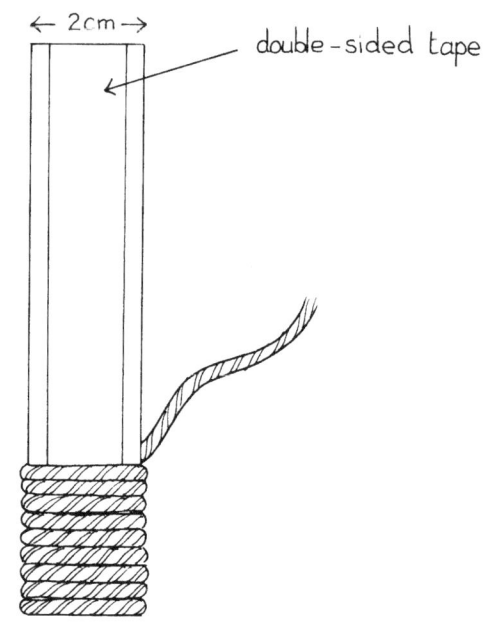

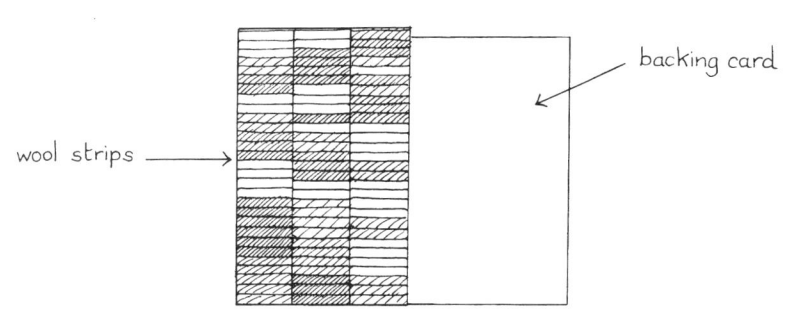

Biblical application

The RE in this activity happens in the research, and in the informal discussion about the choice of colours and the nature of the events. Wool wrapping could be done on a story such as the stilling of the storm or on a character such as Joseph, Ruth, David or the lame man who was healed. Any life which is eventful or has changes of circumstance is suitable for this technique. With a long story such as Joseph, pupils can each be given a short piece of card and one episode of the story. The finished wool windings can be stuck together by placing double-sided tape across a larger piece of thick card and pressing the finished windings to it.

Masks

The Joseph story: Genesis 37; 39—45
Esther: The Book of Esther
The betrayal: Matthew 26.47–56; Mark 14.43–52; Luke 22.47–53; John 18.1–11

Description of the activity

There are many different ways of making masks: this activity uses plain paper plates. Take a plate and draw in the centre the expression of the character it is representing. The plates can be different characters, or one character at different points in the story.

Cut out eyes, mouth and nose. Paper, fabric, wool, tissue, etc., can be applied to give texture and to create features and expression. The masks can be mounted on sticks and used in drama (see page 107, *Story and Drama*), or displayed with writing on feelings (see page 40, *Writing and Poetry*).

NOTE: Use long art straws doubled for sticks as these are safe.

Biblical application

Masks used in combination with dance are an effective way of expressing a biblical story. They help pupils focus on facial expression and meaning. Pupils could take a story such as Judas's betrayal of Jesus, or Esther or Joseph, and select a character at a particular moment, representing them with a mask. The mask should express the person's character, or their reaction to the events of the story. Pupils may wish to work on a character as a group and make a series of masks for the one character so that the whole story can be told using a variety of masks. To do this, the story needs close examination so that the different reactions of the person can be captured in the masks.

NOTE: Joseph is a very long story. Choose a rewritten, shortened version.

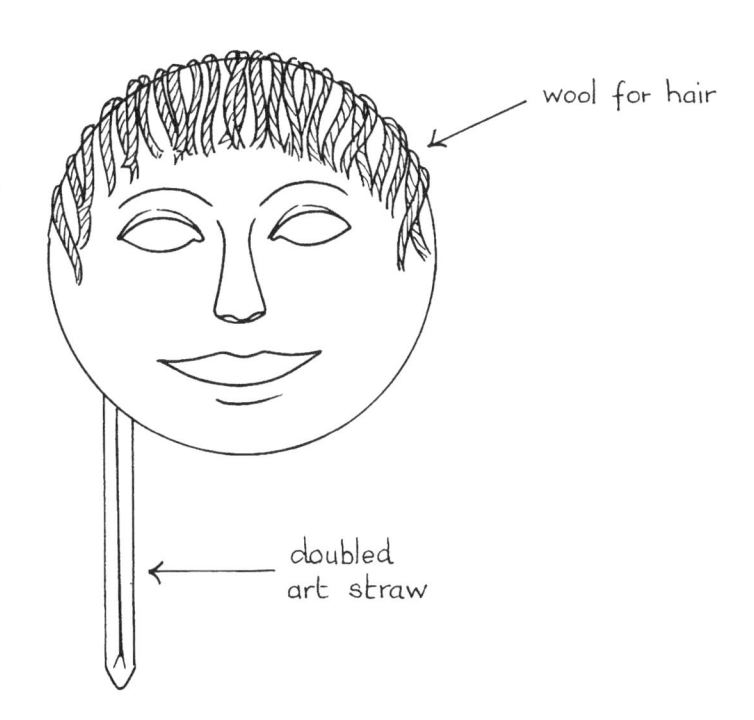

Diorama

Elijah and the ravens: 1 Kings 17.1–6
Peter walking on the water: Matthew 14.29–30
Zacchaeus: Luke 19.1–10

Description of the activity

Two-dimensional landscapes and seascapes can be created from card. Mountainous seas, rolling hills, and the like are cut from card and painted or printed. The finished pieces are then placed one behind the other to form a scene. To make the card stand upright, a small portion should be left blank at the bottom and cut and folded as shown.

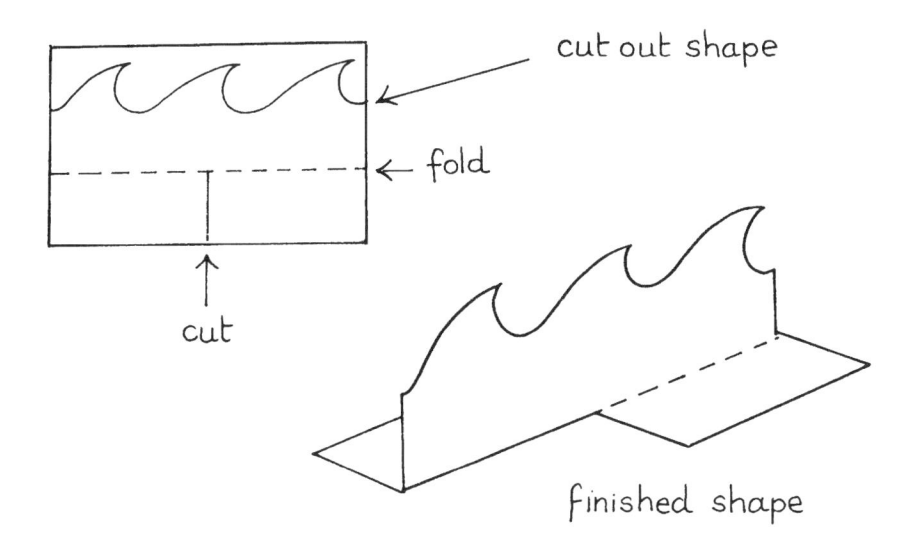

The scene can be placed in a shoebox to form a diorama. A peephole cut in one end and a hole to let in light at the top enable people to view the scene. The technique gives a three-dimensional effect which enables pupils to express the nature of the scene.

Biblical application

This technique creates effective landscapes which can be used for almost any Bible story. Figures can be placed within the landscapes. The three-dimensional effect allows pupils to express the relationship between people by the way they are positioned within the scene. The diorama form allows pupils to communicate the mood of a scene, such as the violence of a storm in the story of Peter, or of someone isolated or at a distance from the crowd in the stories of Elijah and Zacchaeus.

Pupils should try to capture the meaning of the events that took place in each location by their positioning of characters, and their use of colour, and of proportion.

DETAILED ACTIVITIES

Posters

Ask, seek, knock: Matthew 7.7–12; Luke 11.9–13
Watch what you fill your mind with: Philippians 4.3
Seven things God hates: Proverbs 6.16–19

Description of the activity

Making posters is an activity which can be done in most classrooms with very few facilities. Mixed methods can be used: for example, collage and felt pen, calligraphy, and magazine cut-outs. Posters should be clear and eye-catching, and should make a point quickly and easily. Before making their own posters pupils should have an opportunity to look at, and analyse, a variety of commercially produced posters.

An example

Andrea Lacey and Lynn Glove, Rainey Endowed School, Magherafelt, Northern Ireland

Biblical application

Posters can be an effective way of emphasizing certain aspects of a Bible story or biblical teaching. One example, using mixed methods, would be to combine pictures cut from magazines and calligraphy. Pupils letter around pictures which illustrate a biblical idea, following the contours of the illustrations. The lettering could be a comment on those pictures or part of the Bible itself. Posters can be arresting by unusual use of images and words which convey a message. Sections of the Sermon on the Mount (Matthew 5—7) would be suitable for posters, as well as sayings from the book of Proverbs or from the New Testament such as Luke 18.24–25 or parts of Paul's letters. Posters can be interpretative or descriptive but whichever form is used the meaning of the saying or story should be discussed first and pupils should be encouraged to express the meaning as well as depict the images.

ART

Silhouettes and cameos

The fiery furnace: Daniel 3
The crucifixion: Matthew 27.32–50; Mark 15.21–41; Luke 23.26–49; John 19.16–42
Jonah and the worm: Jonah 3.1—4.11

Description of the activity

Silhouettes are black pictures often on a white background, cameos are white on a coloured background. Simple shapes are the most effective for this, such as a black cross against a water wash background or a white dove on a plain background. Pupils can select plain significant items from a story and represent them as cameos or silhouettes. It is as important to think about the background, as it is to make the silhouette, for this will create the "mood" of the picture. Techniques such as water wash, spatter prints, and sponge printing can be used for the background (pages 45 and 61). Silhouettes or cameos and their background can also be created on the computer using a computer paint system and either black or white as the fill colour for the shapes. The various tools (spray, wash, etc.) can be used for the background.

Biblical application

Read a biblical story with the pupils and discuss the meaning. Ask the pupils to choose a significant image to draw. These images, made in silhouettes or cameos, can be placed against suitable backgrounds. A stark crucifixion scene can be made by placing a silhouette of a hill and three crosses against a water-washed background of purples and greys. A very different picture is created by placing a silhouette of Jonah's plant against a background which suggests a burning sun. A silhouette of the fiery furnace can be made against a fiery marbled background.

Cards

The birth of Isaac: Genesis 21.1–7
The great feast: Luke 14.16–24
The prodigal son: Luke 15.11–32
Pentecost: Acts 2.1–13

Description of the activity

Cards are sent on many different occasions: to say sorry, to invite people to a party, to say thank you, and so on. Lots of different art techniques can be used to create cards which will express various sentiments. Cards can be printed (pages 60–61). Rubbings can be made and cut out and applied to a card (page 41). Marbling can be cut up to make small collages for cards: for example, a rising sun for an Easter card (page 38). Pop-up cards can be made or cards can have flaps and sides which reveal hidden messages or pictures. Pupils should have time to see a variety of commercially produced cards before making their own.

An example

> To my dear friends,
> I just want to thank you for taking me to Jesus.
> Without you I would still be paralysed and I couldn't have written the letter.
> I am sorry about the trouble I caused. I know you nearly lost your carpentry jobs because you had to have half an hour.
> I hope you didn't strain your backs lifting me up on to the roof.
> I couldn't believe it when I just stood up and walked away.
> I cannot thank you enough. Without you this could not have happened. Jesus made me run and walk. I feel like everyone else.
> Thankyou
> your dear friend
> Hannah

Hannah Gibbins, Myrtle Springs School, Sheffield

ART

Biblical application

Commercially produced cards can also be collected and analysed for the images they use on Christmas and Easter cards. Old Christmas cards can be collected and classified according to the way in which the nativity scene is drawn: sentimental, classical reproduction, cartoon, etc. Which are the most popular? Why? Images of Mary and Joseph can be discussed. Cut out as many different pictures of Mary as possible and make them into a display. What are the different pictures saying about her? Do they reflect the original story?

Pupils can design their own cards for Christian festivals using a variety of art techniques or computer graphics. In each case, the story on which the festival is based should be read and discussed. The card does not have to be a picture of the story: it can be a more abstract probing into the meaning of the story, or a symbol. For example, a flame can be created on the computer for Pentecost, an exploding cross for Easter.

"Thank you" and "sorry" cards can be made for individuals in stories. What would the prodigal son have written in a "sorry" card to his father? Cards can also be made for "sorry" and "thank you" prayers.

Invitation cards can be made for parties such as the party at the end of the story of the prodigal son or the parable of the great feast. A birth announcement card could be made for the birth of Isaac, or Samuel. These cards should reflect the feeling of the parents. What comment would Abraham and Sarah have written inside?

Printing

Creation: Genesis 1.1—2.25
Ruth and Boaz: 2.1—4.22
The parable of the weeds: Matthew 13.24–30

Description of the activity
Card prints

Prints can be made from thick cardboard by attaching cardboard shapes to a block, coating them in paint, and printing with them.

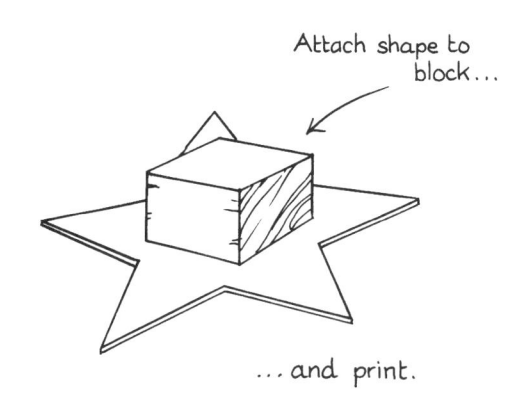

DETAILED ACTIVITIES

Sponge prints
Sponges can be used to cover large areas. They can also be used to print over stencils. To do this, a basic shape, such as a hillside or cloud, is torn or cut from paper; then the sponge is dipped in paint and pressed round the edge of the stencil. The paper stencil is then removed.

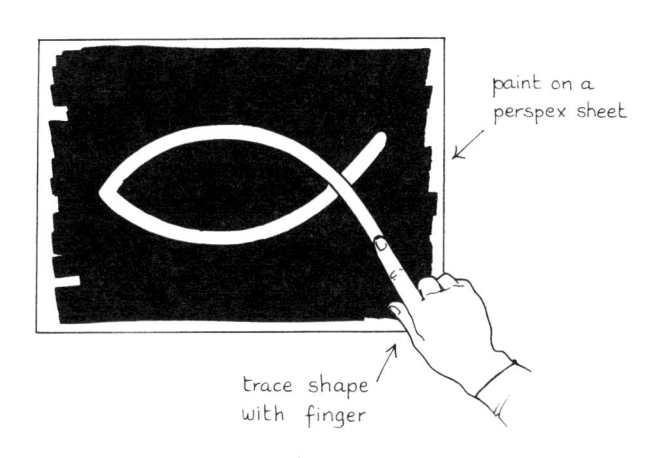

Monoprints
Monoprints involve painting a formica table top or perspex sheet, drawing in the paint with a finger or a tool, then placing a sheet of paper over the paint, pressing it lightly with a dry cloth and lifting it. The paint can be "combed" for a wave effect. A rag or brush can be dipped in another colour paint and used to draw on the formica. Remember the prints will be "mirror style".

Glue and string prints
PVA glue can be dribbled onto card in a pattern, left to dry, painted and used to print with. String can be glued to card and used in the same way. Both of these can also be used for rubbings (see page 41).

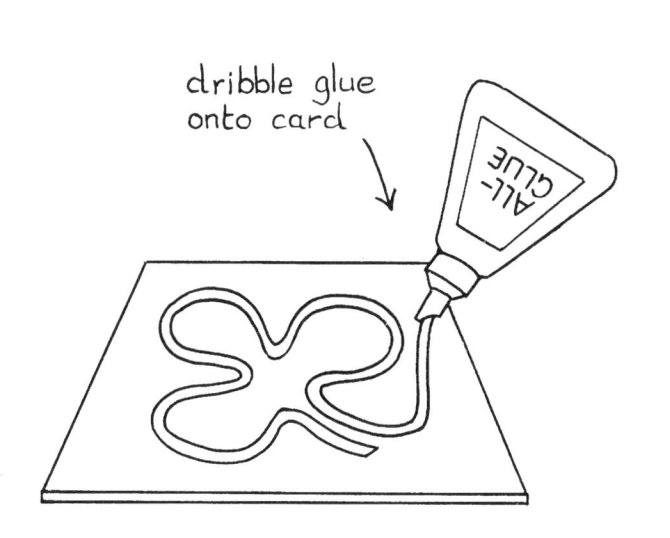

Biblical application
The pupils should read the biblical story first and discuss its meaning. The method of printing selected should suit the story and help to convey meaning. In the story of Ruth, the sun can be created with a glue print to give an enormous swirling sun which will express the conditions Ruth was prepared to accept in order to help Naomi: working in the fields in tremendous heat. Glue prints and string prints can be used for printing basic shapes, such as corn in the story of

ART

Ruth or in the parable of the weeds. A wheatfield can also be printed quickly using a string print of wheat.

Symbols can be drawn in paint for monoprinting (see pages 67–70), but their meaning should be discussed first. Whole landscapes can be monoprinted by painting directly onto the table with a brush then taking a print off the paint.

A variety of printing methods can be used to express the variety and beauty of creation: sponge printing for mountains, water, and sky; monoprinting for sun, moon, and stars; card printing for flowers and animals.

Costumes

The nativity story: Luke 2.1–20; Matthew 1.18—2.12
Pentecost: Acts 2.1–13
Esther: The Book of Esther

Description of the activity

The design of costume in order to express meaning and role is a field of art seldom explored in school. Too often the characters in the school nativity play develop no further in costume than children wearing dressing gowns and tea towels.

The design of simple costumes for a play can be part of the pupils' art and RE experience. Emphasis should be on designing costumes which reflect character and role. Pupils can explore the effect of colour, texture, and style in their designs, and research the type of costumes worn at the time.

As well as replica costumes, pupils can design more "abstract" costumes for drama or dance. What would a costume for "fire" be like for a dance of Pentecost? How could the power of the wind be captured or suggested in a costume?

An example
Esther

Esther wore these clothes because:

- She wanted to look respected
- She wanted to look bright and elegant like on the Clothes Show
- fabric for her dress
- She thinks she looks pretty
- colours for her dress

DETAILED ACTIVITIES

Biblical application

Costume design is a good way of exploring Bible stories. The shepherds would have been dressed in a way that showed that they were poor and outcasts. Mary could be dressed in a way that reflected her character and her role in the story, as well as wearing something which was authentic. Esther would need to be dressed differently at various points in the story to reflect her role and her feelings. The role and character can be expressed by choice of colour and fabric. Scarlet, for example, would make a different statement about Mary from deep maroon.

The story should be studied first, and then each group or individual should select one character to study. After due discussion, a summary should be made of the person's character and the role they play. A sketch should be made of the character and a costume designed. Colours can be indicated by:

colouring in the drawing;

placing patches of colour around the drawing with lines to indicate where these colours would be used;

attaching tiny swatches of material to the edges of the finished drawing.

The pupils' comments around their drawings can become the basis for conversation. For example: "Why would Esther want to look respected?"

Not all drawings have to be made into finished costumes. School expenses and pressure on time often prohibit this. The design itself, however, is useful for exploring the story. If it is possible to make a costume at the end of the exercise this can be rewarding, even if an adult makes the costumes based on pupil designs.

Some useful books:
How They Lived in Bible Times by
   G Jones and R Deverell
   (SU, 1992)
Living in the Times of Jesus of
   Nazareth by P Connolly
   (OUP, 1993)
The Lion Encyclopaedia of the Bible
   (Lion, 1986)
Costumes of Old Testament Peoples
   by P J Watson (Batsford, 1987)

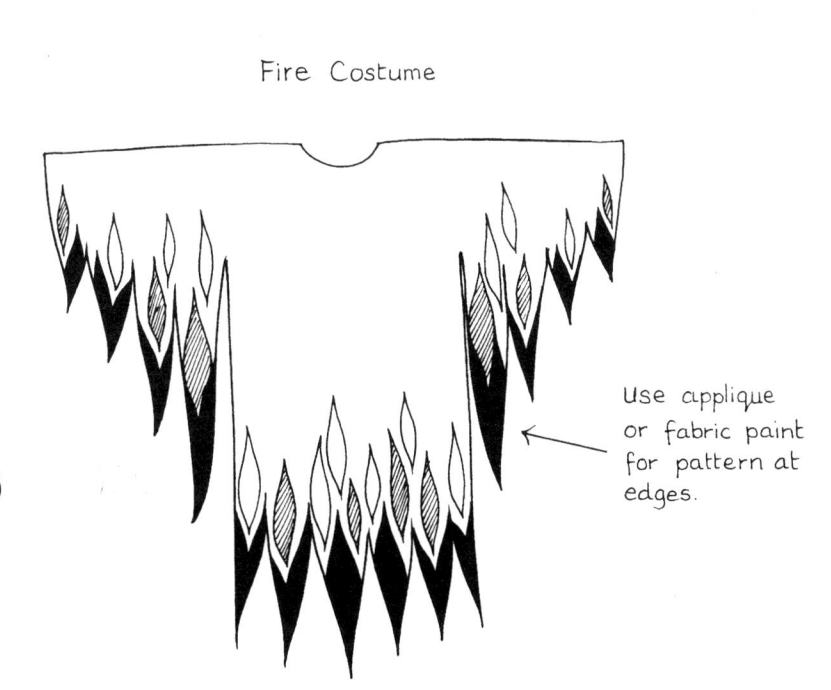

Fire Costume

Use applique or fabric paint for pattern at edges.

Weaving

Crossing the Red Sea: Exodus 13.17—14.31
Paul on the road to Damascus: Acts 9.1–19
Stilling the storm: Matthew 8.23–27

Description of the activity

Materials of a variety of textures can be woven: wools, crepe paper, strips of fabric, ribbon, tissue, and paper. Paper weaving is simple and good for exploring colour. For this, a paper shape is cut by folding the sheet in half and snipping several times across the fold but not right to the edge. Open out the finished shape. Strips of paper can then be woven across. The paper used for weaving need not be plain: it can be cut from magazines, or the paper can be printed or marbled.

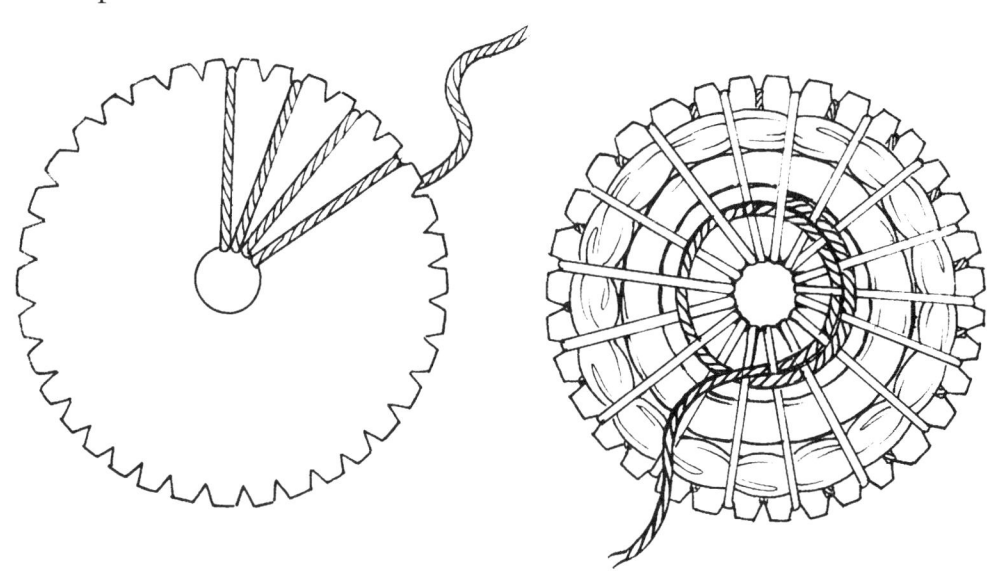

Cardboard can be used as a frame for weaving. Notched paper plates make a good circular frame. Weaving does not have to be in straight or complete lines. Irregular weaving can create expressive backgrounds and landscapes.

Biblical application

Weaving can express events and emotions in biblical stories. After telling the story of the stilling of the storm, half the pupils can be asked to express the storm in weaving and the other half can express the peace. Pieces of weaving should be small to begin with (if using wool) or pupils get discouraged. Emotions such as fear and joy in the crossing of the Red Sea can be expressed in paper weaving, texture and colour being important in communicating this feeling. The light which blinded Paul can be expressed in circular weaving. The words Paul heard can be written round the edge of the circle after it is mounted.

DETAILED ACTIVITIES

Symbols

The Christmas story: Luke 2.1–20; Matthew 1.18—2.12
Easter: Matthew 27.27–50; Matthew 28.1–7
Noah: Genesis 6.1—9.17

Description of the activity

Symbols are very simple shapes which can be used in a variety of ways. They can be incorporated into pictures, as they were in the Middle Ages, so that the observer learns to "read" a picture according to the symbols it contains. Details of some of these symbols are given on the pages listed below. As the shapes are simple and uncluttered, they can be used in many ways:

Printing (see page 60)

Rubbings (see page 41)

Banners (see page 35)

Stained-glass windows (see page 37)

Simple symbolic shapes can be cut from card, stuck to a larger block, painted, and used for printing. A perspex sheet (or formica table top) can be painted and the symbols traced in the paint with a finger. Prints can then be taken from this with paper (newsprint works best). String can be stuck to a block in the shape of a symbol and used for printing. The shape of a symbol can be drawn lightly in pencil, then a line of glue dribbled over the pencil line. When dry, this can be painted and used to print.

A series of stained-glass windows can be made to express the meaning of Easter using symbols (see pages 67–70).

ART

Biblical application

Symbols can be added to biblical pictures to convey meaning. Colour can also be used symbolically by the pupils in their own pictures of biblical stories.

Symbols can be used at Christmas and Easter to create Christmas and Easter trees, the "tree" itself being made from branches planted in a pot. From these trees can be hung symbols appropriate to the festival. Pupils might like to read the Christmas or Easter story and decide on some symbols which arise naturally out of the story, such as the crown of thorns. Traditionally, the majority of the symbols should be made in white and gold. They can be made from card and hung from the branches. Time should be given to deciding on which symbols to use, and to considering their meaning in the original story, and their meaning for Christians today.

NOTE: Make sure all plants used are safe, and only use branches cut in pruning.

Symbol dictionary

Symbolic colours

White or gold:	innocence, holiness, and purity. Used at Christmas and Easter in particular.
Dull yellow:	jealousy, treason, deceit.
Violet:	love, truth, passion, suffering. In the West, it is used in Advent and Lent.
Red:	martyrdom, love, hate, power, the Spirit. Used at Pentecost.
Purple:	royalty, imperial power. Used of God the Father.
Green:	spring, the triumph of life over death, charity, hope. Used generally.
Grey:	ashes, humility, mourning.
Brown:	renunciation of the world, spiritual death.
Blue:	heavenly love, the traditional colour worn by the Virgin Mary.
Black:	solemnity, negation, sickness, and death.
Black and white:	humility and purity.

Symbols

The Church

The ark or a boat
A symbol of the Church. Inside all are safe even if the waters are rough.

The rock
A people with their faith built upon the "rock" of Christ.

© 1996 Bible Society. This page may be photocopied for classroom use only.

ART

God the Father

The all-seeing eye
The ever-present, all-knowing God.

The hand of God
People are sometimes pictured inside a hand. This is a symbol of God keeping safe those who trust in him.

Jesus

The lamb and banner
The lamb was a symbol of sacrifice, the banner a symbol of victory – so together, the victory of sacrificial love.

The phoenix
This is a legendary bird which rises out of its own ashes. A symbol of the resurrection.

The chi-rho
This is the first two letters of Jesus' name in Greek superimposed.

The fountain
This is a water symbol, indicating the washing clean from sin or wrong.

The anchor cross and the chi
The chi was an early symbol of Jesus. The anchor is always shown making a cross shape. This cross was used to express the undeserved love of God.

The Holy Spirit

The nine-pointed star
The fruits of the spirit (Galatians 5.22, 23): love, joy, peace, patience, kindness, goodness, faithfulness, gentleness, self-control.

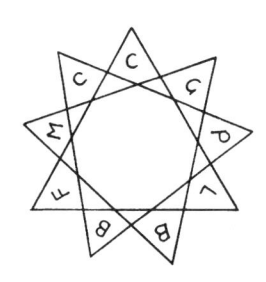

The dove
This is seen as a symbol of the Holy Spirit at the baptism of Jesus.

© 1996 Bible Society. This page may be photocopied for classroom use only.

DETAILED ACTIVITIES

The sevenfold flame
The tongues of fire from Acts 2. The seven represents the gifts of the Spirit: wisdom, understanding, counsel, spiritual strength, knowledge, true godliness, reverent fear (awe).

The Trinity

The trefoil (leaf made of 3 leaflets)
The shamrock, which has a leaf divided in three, was said to have been used by Saint Patrick to explain the Trinity.

Three interwoven circles
To show the three persons of the Trinity and their unity.

Christmas

The star of David
Jesus was a descendant of King David. The Messiah or special king was expected to be a descendant of David. Christians believe Jesus was that king.

The Epiphany star
Epiphany is the time when the coming of the wise men is celebrated. The word "epiphany" means "showing".

The lily
A symbol of the angel announcing the news to Mary. It is the symbol of both Mary and Gabriel.

The Christmas rose
A symbol of the nativity. An unexpected blossom in the middle of winter.

There are many other symbols which can be used for Christmas, such as the crown and some symbols of Jesus.

Easter

Apple
A symbol of salvation. It started as a symbol of wrong in Eden but became a symbol of wrong put right.

© 1996 Bible Society. This page may be photocopied for classroom use only.

ART

Holly
A symbol of suffering and crucifixion.

Ivy
A symbol of eternal life because it is always green.

Laurel
A symbol of victory. Given to athletes when they won a race. A symbol of Jesus' victory on the cross.

Pomegranate
The hope of immortality and resurrection symbolized by the seeds.

The cross and crown of thorns
Good Friday.

The Russian Orthodox cross
This cross has three horizontal bars. The first is the title nailed above Jesus, the second is the bar of crucifixion, the final one is the foot rest which is tilted up towards the repentant thief and down towards the thief who taunted Jesus.

The Calvary cross
This cross stands on three steps, which represent faith, hope, and love.

© 1996 Bible Society. This page may be photocopied for classroom use only.

MUSIC

Colin Humphreys and Philip King

INTRODUCTION

Background

The music section of this book aims to provide teachers with a range of ideas for practical music activities, based around biblical themes and stories. The activities should help pupils understand further some aspect of RE, but they are also designed to have clear learning objectives in music, drawing from the main national curriculum themes of performing, composing, and listening.

The successful integration of RE with music will be achieved through ongoing discussions between pupils and teachers. For example, asking questions such as "How can we represent the parting of the Red Sea in sound?" or "How do you think the Israelites felt when they saw the waters part?" will help to further the pupils' understanding of both RE and music.

Similarly, children composing their own piece for Palm Sunday will need to discuss what made people joyful, when Jesus entered Jerusalem and what qualities make music joyful.

Many teachers find it useful to relate listening activities to practical activities. So, for instance, if the children have just invented a piece about the creation, they might go on to listen to a small part of Haydn's *Creation*. Likewise, work on processional music for the journey into Jerusalem could be followed by the Palm Sunday music from *Jesus Christ Superstar*. Examples of music for listening are included on pages 75–76. Listening in this way is relevant and gives a sense of context.

If you are unsure about leading music activities with instruments, start with a project which just uses voices until you gain in confidence (see "The apostles rap" and "Kum by ya"). When you do use instruments, here are some useful tips.

- Explain the activity before the pupils handle the instrument. Getting their attention when they have the instruments in their hands is difficult!
- Having one instrument between two makes the activity more manageable.
- Don't have every instrument out for every activity. It sometimes helps if the teacher pre-selects instruments for the task.
- Over a number of projects, try to ensure that each pupil plays a range of instruments.
- Give the instruments out in a planned way, avoiding a free-for-all.
- Have a "stop" call (perhaps a rhythm on a cowbell) for when you want to speak, and make sure pupils put their instruments down while you are talking.

In all practical activities, the emphasis should be on enjoyment and participation. Always value the children's work and praise what they do.

The following symbols are used to represent percussion instruments readily available in most schools:

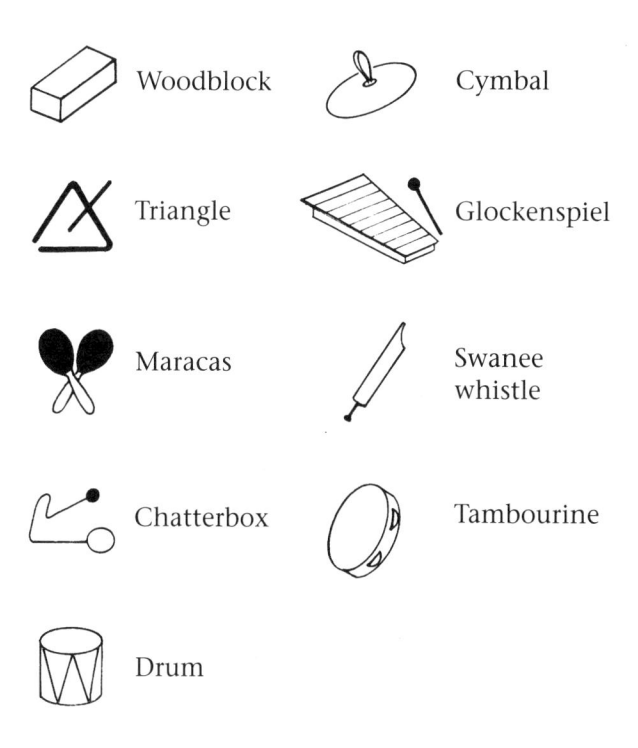

- Woodblock
- Cymbal
- Triangle
- Glockenspiel
- Maracas
- Swanee whistle
- Chatterbox
- Tambourine
- Drum

MUSIC

Resources

Books

Many of these books do not deal specifically with RE topics, but the approaches they promote can easily be adapted.

High Low Dolly Pepper by V Clark (A & C Black, 1990) is a resource book of poems, songs, activities, and games to help the class teacher explore music with young children.

Sound Inventions by R McNicol (OUP, 1992) consists of thirty-two creative music projects for the junior classroom. This book enables the primary class teacher to have the pleasure of exploring music with a class of children.

Music through Topics by V Clark (Cambridge University Press, 1990) listening, discussion, and experimentation are central to the activities described in this book. A sense of humour, enthusiasm, and confidence are important extras for the teacher!

Story, Song and Dance by J Gilbert (Cambridge University Press, 1990) is made up of ten units, each containing material and practical suggestions based on an integrated approach to music, movement, and dance.

Up, Up and Away by D Pearson (OUP, 1987) is a resource collection of songs, poems, games, and activities intended principally for those involved in special schools, but also very useful for teachers in mainstream schools.

Recipes by J Holdstock (Lovely Music (sole distributors), 1992) are three little books with lots of good ideas, including really easy composition ideas producing exciting sounds (hence Recipes!).

Assemblies and music

Music to enter and leave

This can help to create a good atmosphere and a sense of occasion. The following factors should be borne in mind.

- It needs to be varied and appropriate.
- Use a good sound system and reasonable level of volume (faded down at the end – avoid abrupt endings!)
- Be careful about people just talking over the music (wallpaper music).

Opportunities for performing

- Pupils might like to perform a composition from classwork (for a theme in assembly).
- A song learned in class can be performed for the school.
- Pupils receiving instrumental lessons can demonstrate their instrument or a piece they have learnt.
- A parent, member of staff, member of their community or a secondary pupil can perform a piece of religious music or Christian song in assembly.
- All the pupils can experience performance through singing hymns and songs. The singing can be enhanced by suggesting ways of varying the hymns and songs:
  - loud and soft verses
  - some pupils humming an accompaniment
  - a solo
  - a descant
  - some pupils playing recorders or other instruments

Hymn practice

Many schools have a weekly hymn practice. There are several factors to be borne in mind when organizing these.

- How many staff are present? If you have to play and direct, why not let another colleague

(quietly) deal with any discipline problems, so that you can maintain a lively, positive atmosphere.
- Have the music in your head, not your head in the music – if you can!
- Put up clear words on OHP; this encourages good posture.
- Can some of the music also be put on OHP?
- Avoid unnecessary talking – be lively, positive, praising, etc.
- Let pupils listen first – not join in straightaway.
- Is the song or hymn right for the children (both the words and music)?
- Present the song in the most interesting way you can.
- Give the children something to do while you play it through (this will help to maintain interest). They can tap or listen for a certain word or phrase.
- Make sure they understand the words, meaning and mood of the song; for example they might whisper the words to begin with to master the words before attempting the tune.
- Devise activities to teach the rhythm of the words:
    - echo clap the rhythm in phrases
    - clap or tap the rhythm of the words.
- Melody is often the big problem! Here are some suggestions:
    - try to capture the style and mood of the piece
    - make sure you have sung it a number of times before pupils attempt to join in
    - echo-sing phrases from the song
    - look for phrases which are repeated
    - look for phrases which move by steps, by leaps, where there are repeated notes, etc.
    - hum part of the song and then stop and ask where you stopped
    - Move around the room to listen and to praise.
- Make sure the room isn't stuffy.
- Maintain a good atmosphere at all costs – nobody will give of their best if they are "closed inside".
- Keep eye contact with the pupils as much as possible.
- Don't necessarily equate loud singing with good singing.
- Remember the voice isn't at its best first thing in the morning.

Ideas for listening

These lists of pieces of music are by no means exhaustive, but will direct teachers to a range of possibilities in a variety of styles. The teacher will need to listen to the pieces carefully to make sure they are what they really want.

It is usually best to integrate listening to music with other activities, so that it has a context. For example, if you have been studying the story of the creation and invented your own "Creation" piece, then you might go on to listen to Haydn's *Creation*.

Make the extracts fairly short. It helps the pupils to hear the same extract more than once. Always discuss the music with the pupils to help with their understanding. Give them something specific to notice (a mood, an instrument, a musical climax, for example). Some pieces appear in more than one group. This is either because the piece has different sections with contrasting moods, or because some pieces fit more than one category, say sadness and loneliness. Many of these pieces can be a starting point for dance.

Biblical themes

Easter
Bach's *St John Passion* and *St Matthew Passion*: the telling and contemplation of the Easter story
Handel's *Messiah*: "Since by man came death" (salvation); "I know that my Redeemer liveth" (resurrection – reflective); "Hallelujah"

MUSIC

(resurrection – glorification); "Behold and see" (Christ's isolation) and others

The Iona Community, "Easter evening" (from *Enemy of Apathy*, Wild Goose publications), "Jesus is Risen from the Grave" (from *Love from Below*, Wild Goose publications)

Lloyd Webber's *Jesus Christ Superstar*: this contains many items telling the Passion story

Stainer's *Crucifixion*: "Fling wide the gates", for example

Schwartz's *Godspell*: "Oh God, I'm dying", and other pieces

Adrian Snell, *The Passion* (KMC 308)

Christmas

Britten's *Ceremony of Carols*: settings of old English poems about Christmas

Handel's *Messiah*: "For unto us a child is born" and others

Menotti's *Amahl and the Night Visitors*: a short opera about the three wise men

Tippett's *A Child of our Time*: the settings of spirituals are especially appropriate

Old Testament stories

Britten's *Noye's Fludde*: a setting of this Old Testament story as told in the Chester mystery play of this title

H Chappell's "Jazz" series: *Daniel Jazz, Noah Jazz, Goliath Jazz, Jericho Jazz* (Novello)

Copland's *In the Beginning*: a setting of the opening of Genesis

Handel's *Israel in Egypt*: a setting of the story of the Israelites

Haydn's *Creation*: for example, the first chorus about light contains some good dark-to-light effects, and many others

C Hazell, *Holy Moses* (Novello)

J Horovitz and M Flanders, *Captain Noah and his Floating Zoo* (Novello)

M Hurd, *Jonah Man Jazz* (Novello)

Roger Jones, *David* (CMM M20)

Lloyd Webber's *Joseph and the Amazing Technicolor Dreamcoat*

Mendelssohn's *Elijah*: "Baal, we cry to thee", "Draw near all ye people", and others

Vaughan Williams' *Job*

Walton's *Belshazzar's Feast*

New Testament stories

(see also Christmas and Easter)

H Chappell, *Prodigal Son Jazz* (Novello)

Handel's *Messiah*: various items

The Iona Community, "God it Was" (from *Love from Below*, Wild Goose publications)

The Iona Community, "The Son of Mary" (from *Heaven Shall not Wait*, Wild Goose publications)

Roger Jones, *Jairus' Daughter* (CMM M20)

Lloyd Webber's *Jesus Christ Superstar*

Schwartz's *Godspell*: a rock musical

Other religious music

Bach's "Jesu, Joy of Man's Desiring"

Gregorian chant: sacred music sung by monks and choirs

Lloyd Webber's "Pie Jesu" from his *Requiem*

Misa Criola: a South American mass

Missa Luba: a black African mass

Parry's "I was glad": a very powerful opening

Verdi's *Requiem*: "Dies Irae" (Day of Judgement) and others

Vivaldi's "Gloria": a bright song of praise

Music for different moods

The following selection of music is not necessarily religious; it contains pieces of music which capture certain moods: moods which may also be present in biblical stories. The music can be used to explore the mood of a Bible story or be used when exploring a story through dance.

Joy

Beethoven's "Ode to Joy": from the Ninth Symphony (last movement)

Handel's "Arrival of the Queen of Sheba": joyful and majestic

A Menken, *Beauty and the Beast* "Transformation" (Pickwick DST CD458)

Tchaikovsky's "Waltz of the Flowers": dance music with changing moods (reflective, joyful, etc.)

Sadness
Elgar's Cello Concerto (third movement): sad
Grieg's "The Death of Asa" from *Peer Gynt*: very mournful
Lloyd Webber, *Cats*, "Memory" (Polydor 817 810–2)
Saint Saens' "The Swan" from *Carnival of the Animals*: very sad
Verdi's "Chorus of the Hebrew Slaves" from *Nabucco*: sad and oppressed

War
Britten's *War Requiem*: settings of Wilfred Owens' poems – many emotions related to war
Holst's "Mars" from *The Planet Suite*: war music
A Menken, *Pocahontas*, "Savages parts 1 and 2" (Walt Disney Records WDR 7546–4)

Fear
A Menken, *Pocahontas*, "Ship at Sea" (Walt Disney Records WDR 7546–4)
Schubert's "Erl König": a song about fear
Sibelius' *Finlandia*: its dramatic and noble opening can be quite frightening
J Williams, *Jurassic Park*, "The Raptor Attack" (MCA MCD 10859)

Peace and reflection
McDowall's "To a Wild Rose": reflective and gentle
S Myers, "The Deer Hunter, Cavatina" (*Love Themes Point* 2641592)
Pachelbel's "Canon": reflective
Satie's "Gymnopédies": slow, gentle piano pieces

Majesty and nobility
Handel's *Zadok the Priest*: very noble and haughty
Mussorgsky's *Great Gate of Kiev*: very majestic and impressive
Vangelis, "Chariots of Fire", The Themes Album (Emparto EMPR CD 516)
Vangelis, *1492*, "Opening and Conquest of Paradise" (East West 4509–91014–2)

Verdi's "Grand March" from *Aida*: ceremonial
Walton's "Crown Imperial": regal and noble

Anger or storm
Beethoven's Sixth Symphony ("Pastoral"): the storm movement
Mussorgsky's *Night on the Bare Mountain*: towards the end – the beginning is mysterious
Wagner's *Ride of the Valkyries*: stormy and spectacular

Mystery
Debussy's *La Cathédrale Engloutie*: mysterious and majestic
Holst's "Neptune" from *The Planet Suite*: mysterious music

Power
P Doyle, Much Ado about Nothing, Overture (EPIC MOOD CD 30)
R Goodwin, "633 Squadron", *Music from the Movies* (EMI CDMFP 915 CD B7 961212)
Strauss's *Thus spake Zarathustra*: very powerful music
Tchaikovsky's *1812 Overture*: victorious (ending)

The Sea
Britten's *Sea Interludes*
Kachaturian's *Spartacus* (use an extract)

Spring
Vivaldi's "Spring" from *The Four Seasons*
Britten's *Spring Symphony*: a setting of English poems

Fire
Wagner's "Fire Music" from the end of the *Ride of the Valkyries*

Loneliness
Grieg's "Death of Asa" from *Peer Gynt*
Lennon and McCartney's "Eleanor Rigby"
Vaughan Williams' *Sinfonia Antartica*: the desolate sections
H Zimmer, *The Lion King*, "Under the Stars" (Mercury 522690–4)

MUSIC

Music in the Bible

Music played an important part in the secular and religious life of the Hebrew people. This was particularly so during the reigns of David and Solomon, when choirs and instrumentalists became a major part of the worship of the Temple. Secular or religious celebrations were enhanced with music and dance. Miriam danced to tambourines when the Israelites escaped across the Red Sea. Japheth celebrated his military victories with music. David played to Saul to ease his depression.

Music was common at feasts, weddings, and funerals. The mourners had already started playing at the home of Jairus whose daughter had died. Jesus told the people that they were like children playing at weddings and funerals (Matthew 11.17). "We played wedding music for you, but you would not dance! We sang funeral songs but you would not cry!"

The psalms are evidence of the rich musical heritage of Israel. Many were meant to be sung or chanted by choirs. In the Temple, after the fifth century BC there were trained choirs of men and women. Whether there were separate male and female choirs or whether the choirs were mixed we do not know. A number of instruments were used, but the details of these are uncertain.

Psalm 150
> Praise him with trumpets.
> Praise him harps and lyres.
> Praise him with drums and dancing.
> Praise him with harps and flutes.
> Praise him with cymbals.
> Praise him with loud cymbals.
> Praise the Lord all living creatures!
> Praise the Lord!

Stringed instruments

The lyre (kinnor)
A type of wooden lyre which was played with the hand or with a plectrum. It may have been small and portable, and was often used on joyful occasions though it could produce a sombre note for laments.

The harp (nebel)
This was also wooden and plucked with the finger; it was similar to the *kinnor* but with a lower note. David played both the *nebel* and the *kinnor*.

INTRODUCTION

Wind instruments

The pipe (halil)
This was probably a reed instrument, possibly similar to the oboe. Used at festivals and in procession, it was also played at funerals (see Matthew 9.23).

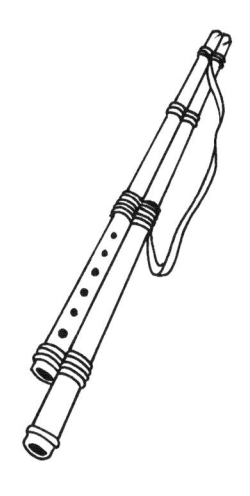

The trumpet (sopar)
The long horn, with an upturned end, that called Israel to war and worship. It is still used in synagogues today.

The metal trumpet (hasosera)
This was essentially a priestly instrument usually made of bronze or silver. It may have been a short straight instrument with a mouthpiece and a cone-shaped or bell-shaped end.

Percussion

Cymbals (selselim)
There were two types of cymbal. One consisted of two metal plates struck together; the second was more like a pair of cups. One was held stationary and the other was brought down hard against it. Cymbals were part of religious ceremonies, as illustrated by Psalm 150. St Paul likens people who have not love to a cymbal: all noise.

Tambourine (top̄)
This was struck by the hand and was often associated with joyful dancing as in the case of Miriam (Exodus 15.20). It was an instrument of celebration rather than one used in formal worship at the Temple, although it could accompany songs of praise. Unlike a modern tambourine it had no bells around it.

MUSIC

Ten music activities

(1) Colouring words

With the class sitting in a circle, discuss with them how they speak when they are happy. Go round the circle with each pupil in turn saying their own name in a happy voice. Now change the mood to one of sadness and repeat the game. Discuss other moods: fear, being fed-up, anger, for example, and ask the pupils to reflect these moods in their voices. Tell a story from the Bible. Ask the pupils to select a character from the story and say in the appropriate voice one sentence or phrase the character may have said.

(2) No copying

Use four flash cards from the "Joshua and the Battle of Jericho" activity (page 95)
(A variation could be having flash cards with other biblical names.) Make sure that the pupils are familiar with four rhythms and that they can see them. One person chooses a rhythm and claps it. The next person follows on with a different pattern. Continue round the circle, remembering that any rhythm can be clapped except the one which has just been heard. This game can also be played using instruments.

(3) Whose voice?

Discuss with the class the story of Eli and Samuel (1 Samuel 3). In particular, consider the importance of listening for a particular voice. Discuss how Christians might listen to God's "voice" today. In what way can people "hear" God. What difficulties might a Christian have today listening to God's "voice"? Discuss the idea of listening to an inner voice. Talk about the difficulties Samuel had. The difficulties of listening and distinguishing voices or sounds can be demonstrated by a simple listening activity. Ask three pupils to stand behind a screen and let them each say the same phrase. Let the rest of the class decide whose voice it is. This can also be done with three instruments played behind a screen (or hidden in some way). Start with three very different ones (shaker, scraper, and woodblock) and progress to three very similar ones (three different shakers).

(4) Music from many cultures

Children enjoy hearing and singing music from many cultures. Try to obtain recordings and/or music of Christian songs from four or five other places, such as Africa, Israel, Spain, America, and Greece. (See the listening list for ideas, pages 75–76.) Let the children listen to them and sing them if they can. Try to encourage an understanding of how the Christian faith is expressed in the music of various cultures. Talk in simple terms about the characteristics of the music (speed, rhythm, words, etc.). Christian songs from a variety of cultures can be found in *Many and Great* and *Sent by the Lord* (Wild Goose) and *World Praise* (Marshall Pickering).

(5) Chanting

Read the story of Elijah, and of how he encourages the crowd to call on their god. Discuss some suitable chants which the pupils could say as the story is read. Get them to construct a piece which uses these chants. Try to make sure that they *gradually* get louder and louder each time.

INTRODUCTION

(6) The same message?
Let the children hear a wide variety of Christian music, perhaps on the same theme, so that they can talk about the similarities and differences. You might borrow recordings of a piece sung by each of a gospel choir, a cathedral choir, a choral society, a children's choir and a rock group. Talk about the styles of these pieces, where they might be sung, and how effective these people are at getting across their message.

(7) With feeling!
So many times, hymns and songs are sung in assembly as if the pupils were singing a telephone directory! Choose a song which they know well and try to improve its performance by concentrating on the meaning of the words. For example, the song "Every morning early I go down to the sea" has these words "I listen, and I listen, I listen, and I listen". Discuss with the class what you need to do if you're listening ("be very still") and then ask them to sing it again, each time getting softer on the word "listen". When they sing "waves crashing on the shore", make sure the waves "crash" with a rolled "r" sound and a big "sh". Always get the mood of the song from the words.

(8) Only two notes
With chime bars G and E, show how it is possible to make up a two-note tune. Play it to the class and let them sing it. Now ask a pupil to come and compose their own two-note tune (using their own words if they wish or a phrase from a psalm). When they are used to this, you can add another note. E G A. Use single lines from the Psalms such as: "Hear my prayer O Lord" (Psalm 102.1) or "Praise the Lord, O my soul" (Psalm 103.1).

(9) Alphabet orchestra
Discuss with the children the sounds you can make with certain letters. For example, the letter "S" can be sounded in lots of interesting ways:

    sssssssss (long and smooth);

    ss ss ss ssssssss (short bursts followed by a longer sound);

    sssSSSSSSSSSSSSSSSsss (gradually getting louder then softer).

"Conduct" the class and let them respond to your actions. Then let the children take turns at leading, first working as a whole class, then in groups. Now go on to work with other sounds – here are some suggestions:

    ooooh   brrr   ch   mm   wah.

You could try working two sounds together. Don't let your compositions be too long, and don't forget to record some of them.

Once the children are confident with this they can select sounds which will build up the background to a biblical story – the sound of the sea for Jonah; the wind for Elijah when he meets God on the mountain.

MUSIC

(10) Magical movements – using an electric keyboard

This is a particularly exciting game to play in the hall with younger children. On most keyboards, there are buttons to select different speeds and different kinds of music. By pressing these buttons at random every twenty seconds or so, and by pressing down one key on the keyboard, you can provide a wealth of sounds for them to respond to in movement.

This activity also provides an opportunity for you to discuss their responses with the children. Did certain rhythms and sounds make them respond in a particular way? Did they make them feel a certain way? Talk about writing Christian music and discuss with pupils the different rhythms and styles which would be suitable for various Christian songs. If Christians want to express the joy of Easter Sunday, what could they select? If they wanted to express the sorrow of Good Friday what would they select?

DETAILED ACTIVITIES

Procession

David and the Ark: 2 Samuel 6.1–23
The Queen of Sheba: 1 Kings 10.1–29
Jesus enters Jerusalem: Matthew 21.1–11; Mark 11.1–11; Luke 19.28–44; John 12.12–19

Description of the activity

This activity involves pupils creating music for a procession. It is a concept with which pupils may not be familiar, so time may need to be spent in drama exploring different types of procession. Processions can be slow and stately, sad or joyful. Pupils may like to listen to part of Handel's "Arrival of the Queen of Sheba".

MUSIC

The entry into Jerusalem

Read the story of Jesus riding on a donkey into Jerusalem. Discuss this story with the pupils, the type of procession it was, and what the people were expressing when they cried "Hosanna". Pupils can play their own processional piece using the notes G and A on chime bars, glockenspiels, recorders, etc.

Play this piece slowly:
(count: 1 2 3 4 1 2 3 4)
(the dashes after the final G are the counts for the long note)

G G A A G – – –

G G A A G – – –

G G A A G – – –

G G A A G – – –

Some can play the tune while others play the rhythm only.

Now change over so that others have the opportunity to play the tune.
The tune could be changed to:

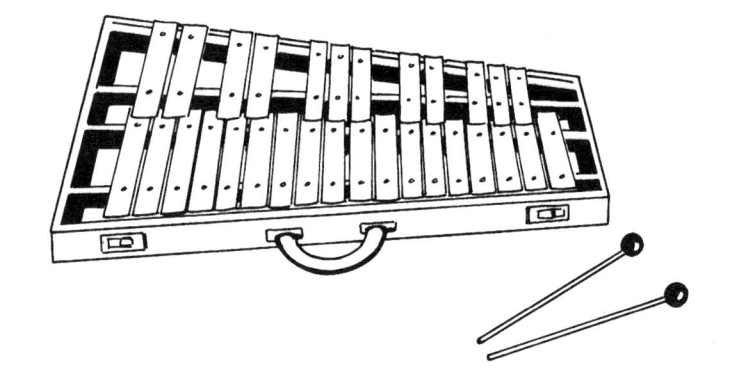

G G A A G – – –

G G A A G – – –

A A G G A – – –

G G A A G – – –

Begin to put an accompaniment to it. Some might play line one and continue. Others might join in at line two, others at line four. This will create the impression of the procession getting nearer.

Using the same idea pupils can work in groups to create their own compositions.

DETAILED ACTIVITIES

Examples

Happy procession (entry into Jerusalem)

🎹 G GA AA AG, x3

1) Play the tune with △ on each note
2) Play the tune alone
3) Play the tune with ◯ on each note
4) End with ♪ crash

Lucy Britton and Claire Redfern, Year 4, Fairfield School, Stapleford

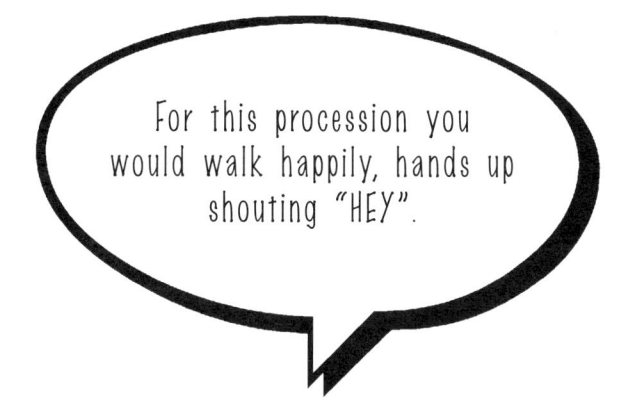

> For this procession you would walk happily, hands up shouting "HEY".

Lucy Brian and Roxanne Pritchett, Year 6, Stevenson School, Stapleford

Sad procession (Widow of Nain's son)

🎹 slowly and heavily GG AA, x3
♩ used on the first three notes each time.

Luke Shiels and James King, Year 4, Fairfield School, Stapleford

> For this procession you would be crying, head drooping down. Walking slowly.

Jonathan Kerr and Daniel Scalan, Year 5, Stevenson School, Stapleford

MUSIC

Biblical application

There are various processions in the Bible: the entrance of the Queen of Sheba, David bringing the Ark into Jerusalem, Jesus entering Jerusalem. There would be funeral processions for the widow of Nain's son (Luke 7.11–17) and Lazarus (John 11.1–44). Pupils should try to capture the mood of each particular procession and express it in music.

Musical stories (1)

Gideon: Judges 6.1—7.25
David and Goliath: 1 Samuel 17.1–58

Description of the activity

This activity looks at a story and describes characters and background in music. Before trying this activity, pupils might like to listen, for example, to some film music for battle scenes, such as the battle scene from Henry V. *Henry V*, "Battle of Agincourt" by P Doyle (EMI Records, CDC 7499192).

David and Goliath

Read the story of David and Goliath and discuss it with the pupils. Discuss the differences between the big, powerful Goliath moving slowly, and small, nimble David. Pupils can make up some music to describe these two characters – perhaps some film music to go with the fight. (For this activity, we will use only the notes C D E G A.)

Discuss with the pupils what sort of melody would best describe Goliath: loud or quiet; fast or slow; high or low. They will probably decide loud, slow and low. Use a xylophone or the deep notes of a piano and ask a pupil to make up a short melody, perhaps using the five or six sounds from the notes which are allowed. This might be very slow, perhaps repeating a note or going back to a note. Make sure the tune can be played again in exactly the same way. Now talk about the music to describe David. Perhaps this might be played on a glockenspiel or chime bars. Ask the same questions as above. The pupils might suggest quiet, fast and high sounds. Again, ask someone to devise a short tune using only five or six sounds from the notes which are allowed. The class can now work in pairs (some may have to use untuned instruments).

Each pair should have two contrasting instruments. They could produce some film music, maybe using the following scene:

Goliath appears on the hillside

David watches from a distance

Goliath comes forward

David taunts Goliath

Goliath becomes angry

...develop the story until Goliath falls to the ground.

An example
David

quickly and lightly

EEAG — EEAG — EEAG

Goliath

slowly, heavily, loudly
C C D E D
C C D E D
    C C C

Kimberley Dinan, Year 6, and Abby Rischer, Year 5, St John's Church of England School, Stapleford

Biblical application
This technique can be applied to any story with two or more strong characters and several scenes. The emphasis should be on interpretation as well as description.

MUSIC

Musical stories (2)

The plagues of Egypt: Exodus 7.14—11.10
The good Samaritan: Luke 10.25–37

Description of the activity

Parts of a story can be represented in music, and using percussion instruments means that most pupils can participate. The story can be read in between the musical representations.

The plagues

Some of these plagues can be represented in music. Different groups could each take one of the following:

River turns to blood
Use metal instruments like glockenspiels, chime bars, and triangles to represent the sparkling running water. Stroking the glockenspiel up and down with the beater makes a good effect.

Now introduce a serious, slow drum beat to show the water turning to blood – the metal instruments could get slower at this point.

Discuss the results together in groups. Did the drum beat improve the effect? When the water turns to blood, would you choose higher notes, lower notes or the same notes?

Plague of frogs
Use scrapers and wood blocks to make jumping effects to represent the frogs. Start with one instrument and gradually introduce more – this will show the number of frogs increasing. Will the music gradually get faster or slower as it progresses? Are there other instruments which would improve the effect?

DETAILED ACTIVITIES

Plague of locusts

Use shakers (maracas, etc.) and tambourines to create a busy locust piece; as with frogs, perhaps start with one instrument and build up from there. Later the instruments can be faded one by one to show the locusts moving into the distance. Will it be best to play fast or slowly to capture the mood of the insects? How can the effect be improved? Could vocal sounds be used to add to the impression of a swarm?

Darkness

Discuss together how groups of sound might represent gloomy darkness. Will the music be fast or slow (or very fast or very slow)? Will it have high sounds or deep sounds? Which instruments would be best for this effect? If a piano was used, which end would be played? Try clusters of notes (a group of notes all close together) and listen to the effect they produce. How would the piece be started and how would it move on and finally end?

Making an extended piece

With the work done so far, make an extended piece with people reading parts of the Bible story to link the different sections.

Further ideas

Sing the well-known song "When Israel was in Egypt's Land, Let my people go." Perhaps pupils could begin and end the extended piece by singing this spiritual.

Let my people go

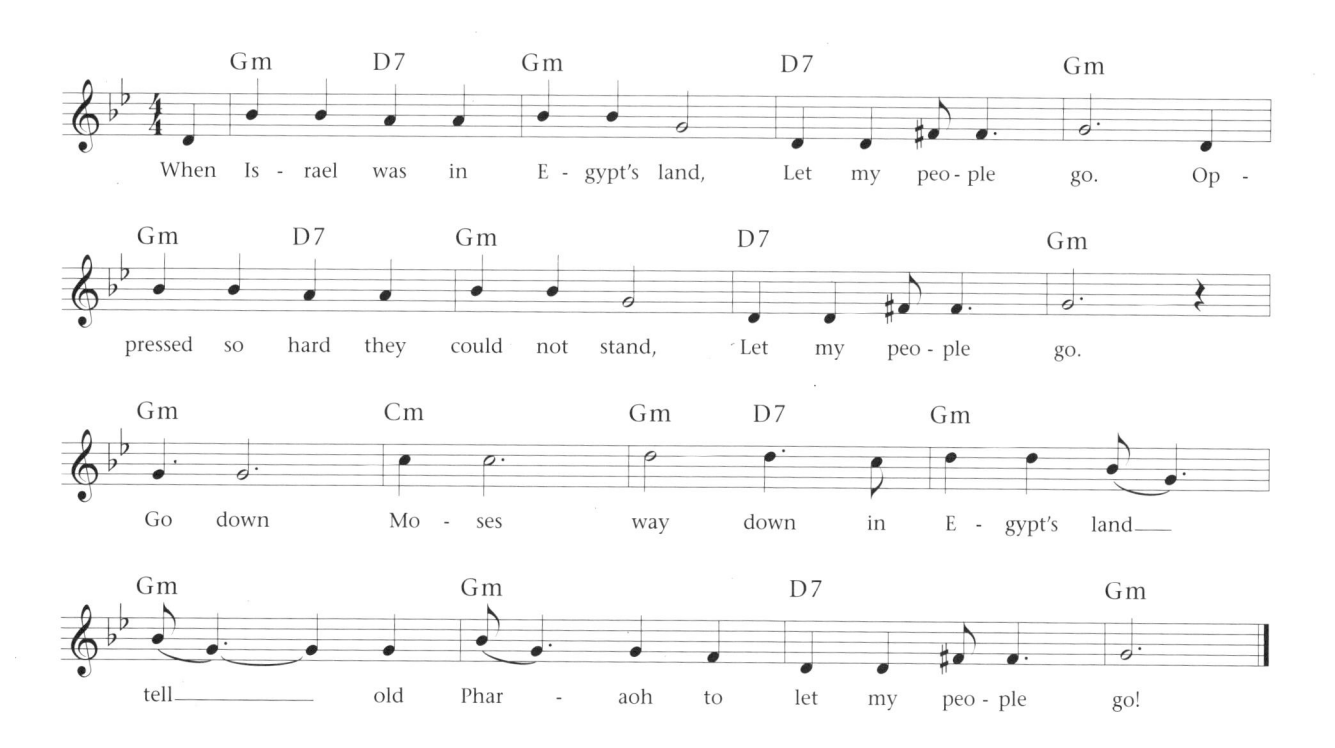

MUSIC

An example
Frogs
 ▱ x 10
 Plus occasional 🥢. More 🥢 at the end.
 Woodblocks played quietly, plus silences at first, then louder and more continual.

Hail
 🎾 x 10 and ▱ x 10, played together.
 Quietly and then more loudly.

River into blood
 Continual running of beaters up and down 🎹: quickly and lightly changing to slowly and loudly.
 Add in beats on the ▱ becoming more frequent.

Ruth Taylor and Daniel Clee, Year 5, Holly Jones and Mark Cureton, Year 6, St John's Church of England School, Stapleford

Biblical application
This activity only works on stories with ingredients that can be easily represented. With The good Samaritan, there are various types of footsteps and the attack. The story of the plagues is an example of a story which makes a good subject for the technique, but the nature of the story means it must be carefully handled. Discuss with the pupils the number of chances Pharaoh was given to let the people go. Why do they think he kept changing his mind? What was the alternative to forcing Pharaoh's hand?

Singing project

Jesus' presence: Matthew 18.20, 28.20b

Description of the activity
This activity explores how songs can be sung with expression, pupils varying volume, speed, and so on to suit the feeling or subject of the song. Before singing, pupils should discuss the verses and decide how they should be sung and why.

Kum by ya
This is a very well known song; however, in case pupils don't know it, it is shown at the end of this section. Each verse lends itself to a special musical treatment.

(1) Kum by ya my Lord, kum by ya.
   Kum by ya my Lord, kum by ya.
   Kum by ya my Lord, kum by ya.
   Oh Lord, kum by ya.

The last line is used in every verse.

(2) Someone's joyful Lord, kum by ya. (three times)
   Oh Lord, kum by ya.

(3) Someone's crying Lord, kum by ya. (etc.)

(4) Someone's praying Lord, kum by ya. (etc.)

(5) Someone's clapping Lord, kum by ya. (etc.)

Perform each verse in a way that expresses the emotions of the words. Ask pupils the following questions.

Should we sing the verse loudly or softly?

Should we sing fast or slow?

Should we sing unaccompanied or add some instruments?

If we add instruments, which ones should we add?

Should we play a regular beat throughout the verse?

Or should we just play on certain important words?

Here is an example of how a group might treat verse 4:

Sing slowly and quietly – to capture the reflective nature of prayer – perhaps a solo voice or small group; the others in the class could hum the tune quietly; play a quiet triangle beat on the syllable 'pray' or the word "praying" each time, and on the word "ya".

Put together a final performance that contains your ideas. ("Kum by ya" is thought to mean "Come by here".)

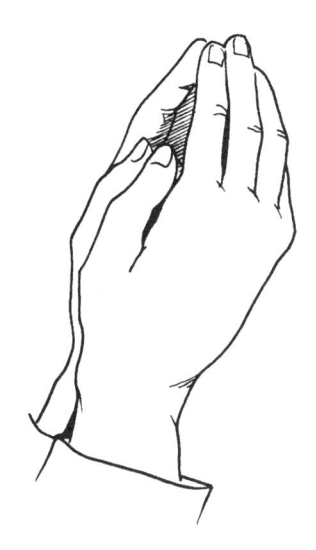

MUSIC

Kum by ya

[Musical notation with chords C, G, F, C, Am, Em, Dm7, G, C, G, F, C, F, Am, G7, C in 3/4 time]

Kum-by-ya my Lord, kum-by-ya. Kum-by-ya my Lord, kum-by-ya. Kum-by-ya my Lord, kum-by-ya. Oh Lord, kum-by-ya.

Biblical application
Many songs, particularly many hymns and modern choruses, are biblically based. Pupils could explore the biblical passage behind the song or hymn.

Musical journeys

Crossing the Red Sea: Exodus 13.17—14.31
Manna: Exodus 16.1–36
Mount Sinai: Exodus 19.1—20.17
Water from the rock: Numbers 19.1—20.21

Description of the activity

Journeys can be of many types, sad, hopeful, joyous or frightened. They can be journeys of escape or journeys of despair, as people travel into exile. The different aspects of a journey and the events which occur during it can be expressed in music.

DETAILED ACTIVITIES

The journey of the Israelites

Read the story of the journey of the Israelites in Exodus and discuss what type of journey this was with the pupils. Give the pupils the map showing the journey of the Israelites or ask them to design their own. This map can be performed as a piece of music by following the arrowheads across the page. The map shows some of the events that happened to the Israelites and these can be represented by musical effects.

These are:

(1) A sound to represent the marching people (perhaps a steady beat on a selection of instruments). This music could be used in between the next three sections. Would the type of marching have changed as the journey progresses? Why?

(2) The crossing of the Red Sea (using instruments which suggest water). When the sea crashed on the Egyptians who are following, you could add some extra effects (some cymbal clashes, perhaps).

(3) Manna raining from heaven (perhaps a rain-like effect on gentle-sounding instruments).

(4) Mount Sinai was an important place, where Moses collected the Ten Commandments. (The music could sound important and grand – perhaps including ten chimes to show the Ten Commandments.)

For each section the teacher should discuss which instruments the pupils are going to use, and how they will play them to get the effect they want. The pupils can play the map – and they will have created their own composition. The piece will be in these sections:

Marching music; crossing the Red Sea – and ending with crashes

Marching music

Manna music

Marching music

Mount Sinai music

Marching music – perhaps fading away at the end

Make a recording of your finished piece.

Further ideas

Read the stories again and see if pupils can find other events in the journey which they could add to your piece. For example, the water from the rock in Exodus 17.

MUSIC

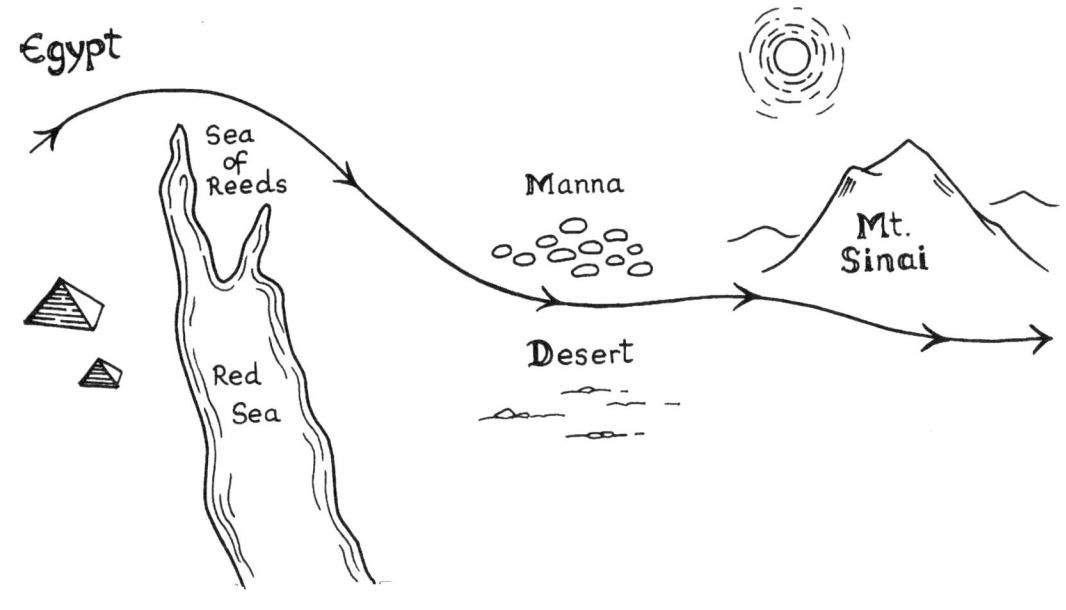

An example
Marching

   A G A G, x 5, regular beat

   keeping time

Red Sea

   x 2, quiet then loud, then bang on them for 5 seconds

   crash

Holly Jones and Mark Cureton, Year 6, Ruth Taylor and Daniel Clee, Year 5, St John's Church of England School, Stapleford

Biblical application
There are many journeys in the Bible. Abraham's was a journey of faith. The exodus was journey of hope towards a promised land. Mary and Joseph's flight to Egypt was a journey of fear.

DETAILED ACTIVITIES

Rhythm (1)

The creation: Genesis 1.1—2.25
The fall of Jericho: Joshua 5.13—6.27
The disciples: Matthew 10.1–4; Mark 3.13–19; Luke 6.12–16

Description of the activity

The activity is to strengthen basic skills in maintaining a rhythm. It could be applied to almost any content. Pupils go through a story and list the key words. These are then clapped to certain rhythms.

Joshua and the battle of Jericho

Read the story of Joshua and his famous battle – Joshua 6.1–27 and discuss the story with the pupils. How do they think the army felt obeying such a strange command? Some of the key words from this story can be used to create compositions.

Pupils should make four flash cards as follows and add the appropriate notes:

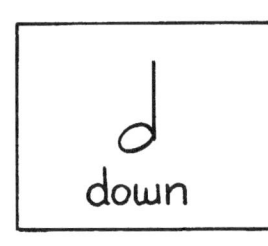

| tumbling | down | Joshua | blow the trumpet |

MUSIC

(1) Using the first two flash cards only, let the pupils chant each one in turn as you hold up the cards. Try to keep the chanting at a steady beat.

(2) Now let the pupils take turns as leader.

(3) Introduce the other flash cards gradually, when pupils have become confident at chanting the first two. (This may be in later weeks, depending on the age or stage of the children.)

(4) Let the pupils each have a strip of paper which they can fold into four:

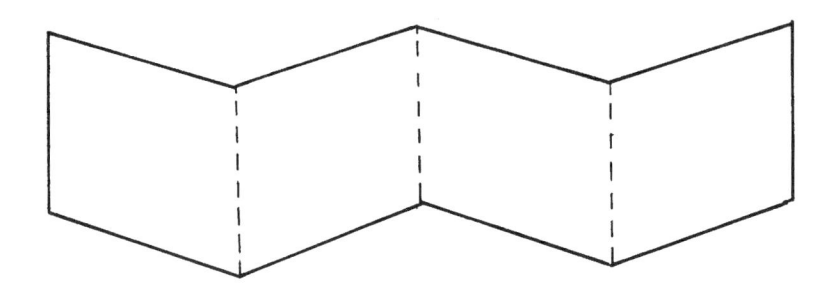

(5) They can now write their own composition using the rhythm patterns they have learned. Here are some possible options (the list is endless):

Joshua | Joshua | tumbling | down

(6) The pupils can then each chant their compositions together at the same time – and they will all fit! You could start everyone by saying:

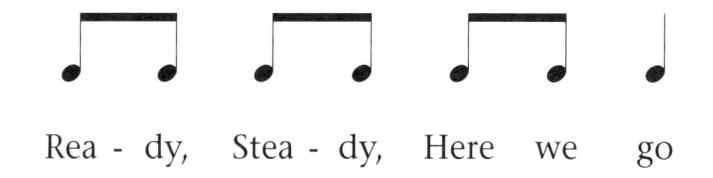

Rea - dy, Stea - dy, Here we go

(7) Now pupils can use a selection of rhythm instruments instead of chanting. It might be helpful to limit the number of people playing (perhaps one instrument between two people and then change over).

(8) When pupils have had lots of practice with this, they could begin to build up a longer composition. Here is one idea:

> Everyone plays their own composition (at the same time)
>
> All those with shakers play
>
> All those with wooden sounds play
>
> One person plays alone
>
> Everyone chants their composition
>
> Everyone plays their own composition

An example

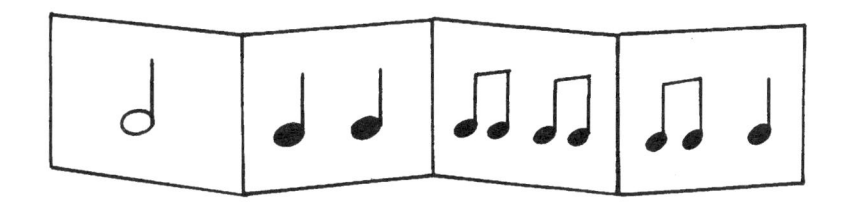

Charlotte Lamb, Year 3, St John's Church of England School, Stapleford

Biblical application
The technique could be used on most stories to master content; it could be combined with others to explore meaning. If key words are listed, these should include words that cover meaning and significance which have come out of discussion, as well as proper names and words which describe events. Rhythms could be created for the disciples' names and for parts of creation.

MUSIC

Rhythm (2)

The feeding of the five thousand: Matthew 14.13–21; Mark 6.30–44; Luke 9.10–17; John 6.1–5

Description of the activity

As in the previous activity, this section aims to develop the pupils' sense of rhythm. The rhythm chosen will depend on the story.

Five loaves and two fishes

For this activity invent a piece of music based on dividing 5 and 2 to emphasize the multiplication of the food.

Pupils choose two contrasting instruments or group of instruments, such as shakers and drums. They can work in pairs or small groups, or as a whole class.

One instrument (one group) invents a rhythm based on 5 (NOTE: This *does not* mean five beats to a bar, which is very difficult). You might choose this rhythm:

The other instrument (or group) invents a rhythm based on the number 2 – two slow beats for example.

Now make a musical dialogue – where the first group plays their ideas, followed by the second group and so on. Perhaps the piece could grow quicker and then slow down again. Perhaps the two ideas could come together at some time. To show how the 5 and 2 multiplied as a result of the miracle performed by Jesus, pupils could expand the rhythms in the musical dialogue.

Here is how a piece might develop (pupils could try this version if they liked – or change it to suit their own ideas):
   Five quick beats on shakers
   Two slow beats on drums
   Five quick beats on shakers – (gap) – then another five quick beats
   Two slow beats on drums – (gap) – then another two slow beats
   Shakers play their rhythm three times in a row
   Both groups play together – getting faster (it doesn't matter if they don't keep the beat steady in this section)
   All slow down
   Five quick beats on shakers
   Two slow beats on drums

Extending this idea

To show how Jesus provided for many people with so little food, one pupil could walk around the room offering food to the players; the players only perform when this pupil comes to them. The teacher could incorporate this idea into the piece above. A narrator could be added to the whole piece, who would tell the story as the music progressed.

An example

Feeding of the five thousand

   (x = 1 shake or beat)

   A x xx x x

   B x x

   Play A five times

   Play B five times

   Play A three times

   Play B three times

   Play A and B together until A has played three times

   Aaron Eames, Emma Thompson, Jacob Bamfold, and Amy Webster, Year 4, Stevenson School, Stapleford

Biblical application

There are various stories which suggest certain rhythms. The five and two of the feeding of the five thousand have been used here. The aim of this exercise is not merely to sustain the rhythm but also to express in its growth, the unfolding miracle.

MUSIC

Rap

The story of Joseph: Genesis 37.1—46.7
The apostles: Matthew 10.1–4; Mark 3.13–19; Luke 6.12–16

Description of the activity

A rap consists of chanting words to a strong rhythmic background. The style comes from West Indian reggae music. Pupils will need to practise rapping the words in order to find out just how the rhythm fits comfortably. The printed rhythm is just a guide – it does not have to be exactly followed. When they have done this, they can set a good automatic rhythm going on an electronic keyboard to give them a background for writing their own rap, experimenting with different rhythms to see which fits best.

The apostles rap

This rap helps the pupils to remember the names of the twelve apostles, or "disciples" as they are often called, and is also great fun!
This work is best done in small groups. Pupils can experiment with this rap.

DETAILED ACTIVITIES

The Apostles rap

Listen ev'rybody to the things that I say,
As we name all the apostles in a special way
There are twelve of these disciples in the following lines;
The followers of Jesus in Bible times
There was Peter, Andrew, James and John,
Philip and Bartholomew and then Simon,
Thomas, Matthew and a second James,
Thaddaeus and Judas were the other names.
And now you know their names through this special rhyme,
Let's go through them one more time;
There was Peter, Andrew, James and John,
Philip and Bartholomew and then Simon,
Thomas, Matthew and a second James,
Thaddaeus and Judas were the other names.

MUSIC

Further work

The pupils in their groups could continue the idea by composing further lines of the rap based on the twelve apostles. For example, additional information could include the facts that:

Peter was originally called Simon;
he denied Jesus three times,
Judas betrayed Jesus for thirty pieces of silver;
Thomas doubted Jesus' resurrection; and so on…

The pupils could look at the book of Matthew for more information on the apostles. The variations are endless. Each group could compose and perform their own rap, but they will need plenty of time to prepare.

An example
The Joseph rap

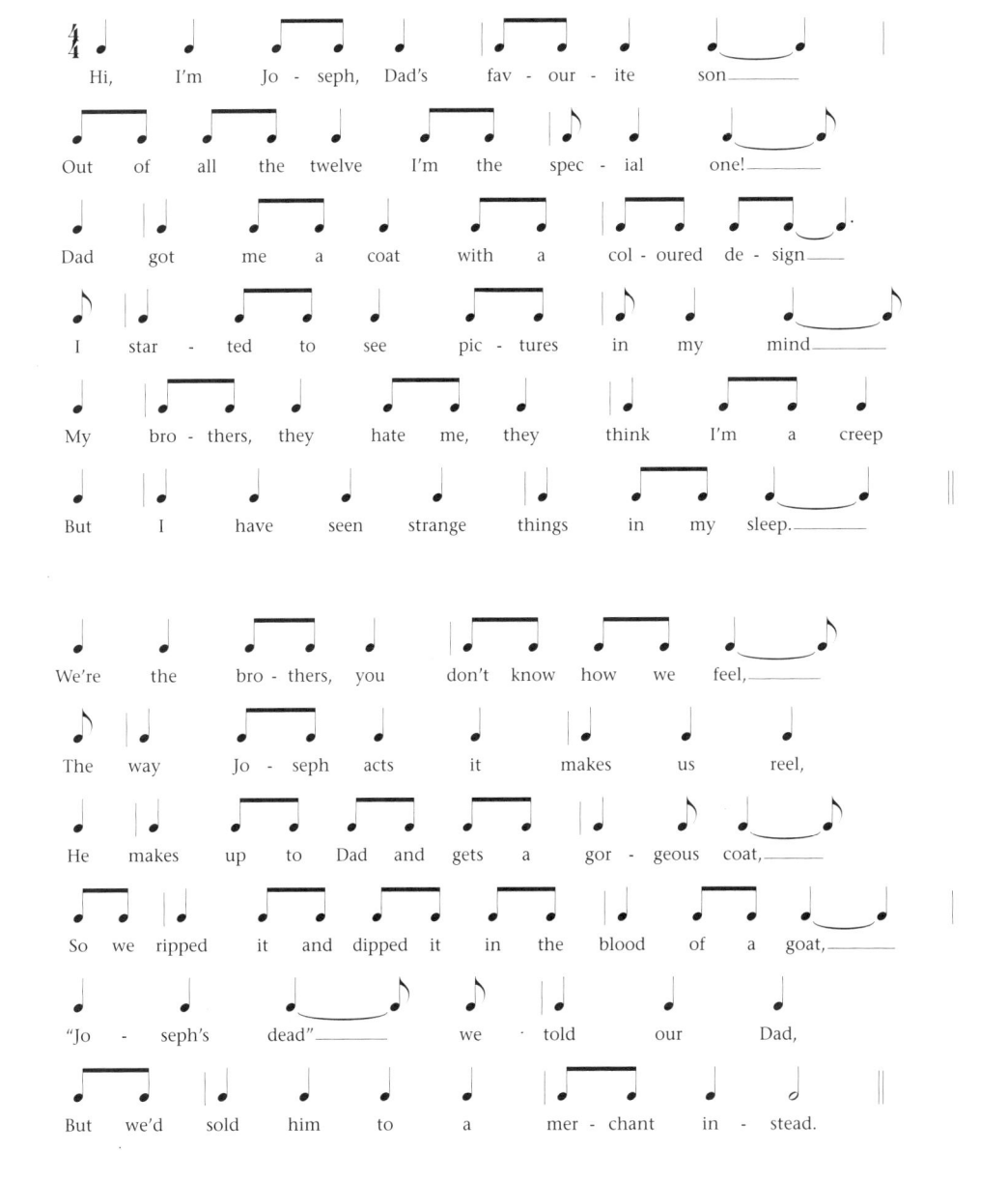

Hi, I'm Joseph, Dad's favourite son
Out of all the twelve I'm the special one!
Dad got me a coat with a coloured design
I started to see pictures in my mind
My brothers, they hate me, they think I'm a creep
But I have seen strange things in my sleep.

We're the brothers, you don't know how we feel,
The way Joseph acts it makes us reel,
He makes up to Dad and gets a gorgeous coat,
So we ripped it and dipped it in the blood of a goat,
"Joseph's dead" we told our Dad,
But we'd sold him to a merchant instead.

DETAILED ACTIVITIES

Hi, I'm Jacob, the father of eleven,
The twelfth's made his journey up to heaven
Attacked by an animal, my favourite child!
Savaged by a lion, or other beast wild.
His beautiful coat caused nothing but grief
When he told the boys about stars in his sleep.

I'm Potiphar's wife and I fancied that Joe
I thought me and him should give it a go,
Joseph's our slave and hunky at that
But he said "no" the stupid rat.
Now he's locked up, I've sent him away,
You don't refuse me and see the light of day!

Pharoah's my name, I love that Joe,
He saved me money when I let him go.
I told him my dream and he saw us slim
When seven fat cows and seven thin
Came out of the Nile, the thin ate the fat,
But they got no bigger, Joseph warned me that

103

MUSIC

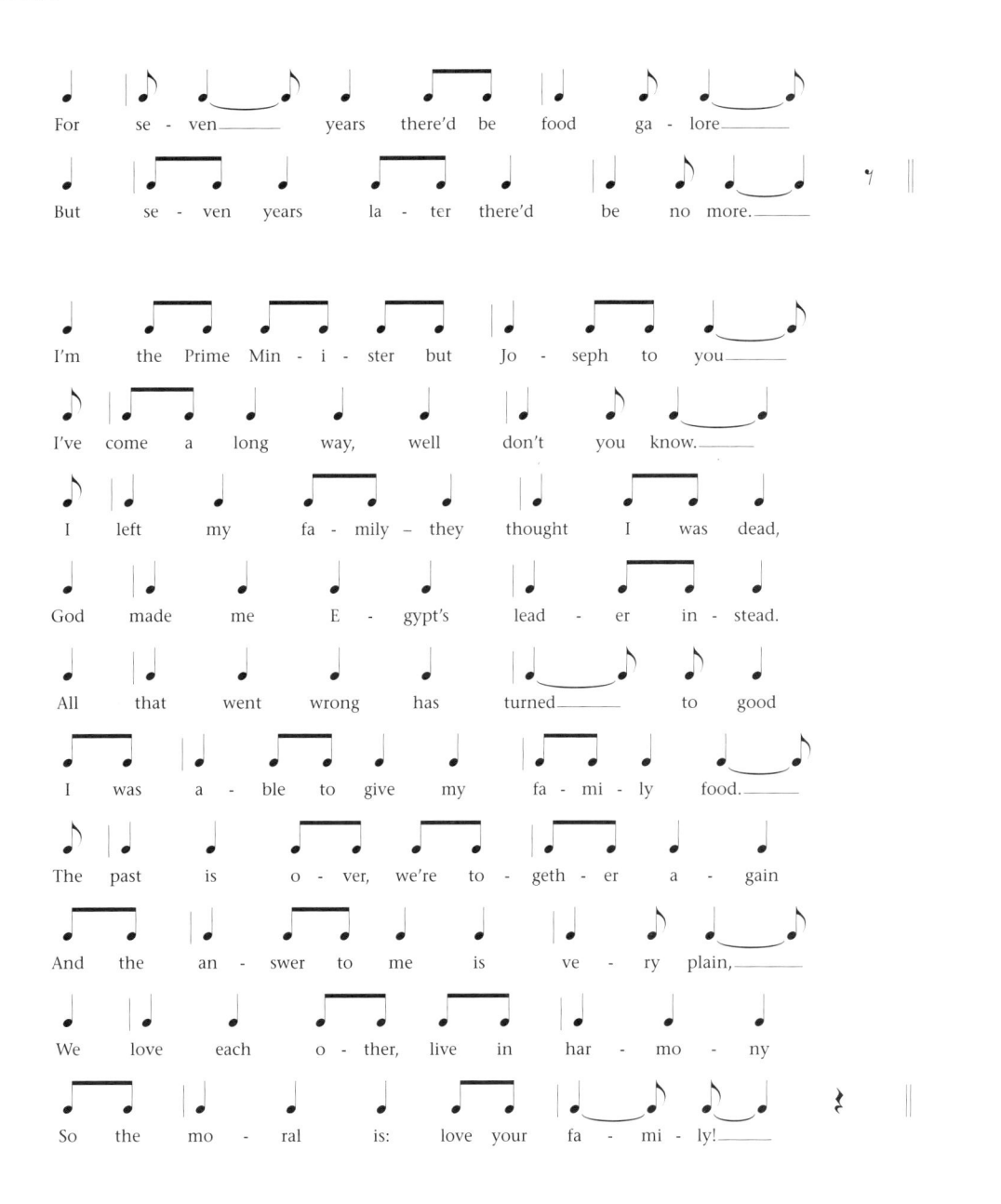

For se - ven years there'd be food ga - lore
But se - ven years la - ter there'd be no more.

I'm the Prime Min - i - ster but Jo - seph to you
I've come a long way, well don't you know.
I left my fa - mily – they thought I was dead,
God made me E - gypt's lead - er in - stead.
All that went wrong has turned to good
I was a - ble to give my fa - mi - ly food.
The past is o - ver, we're to - geth - er a - gain
And the an - swer to me is ve - ry plain,
We love each o - ther, live in har - mo - ny
So the mo - ral is: love your fa - mi - ly!

Heather Wilson, Year 8, Nottingham Girls High School

Biblical application

Rap can be used on most stories. Pupils can write their own raps on biblical stories. The technique "Points of View" (page 32, *Writing and Poetry*) works well for this as it helps pupils see different characters' perspectives.

DETAILED ACTIVITIES

Soundscape (1)

The flood: Genesis 6.1—9.17
Elijah meets God: 1 Kings 19.1–18

Description of the activity

A soundscape is like painting a landscape of a story in sound. The passage is read by a narrator or a group of narrators, while other pupils provide the musical background. Make sure that loud effects do not drown the words – have the words spoken before a loud effect takes place. Before pupils attempt to create a soundscape they should discuss the mood or moods of the story and its message.

In the following passage, the effects shown are suggestions.

Noah

Genesis 7.16—8.5 (some verses omitted)

The Lord shut the door behind Noah.
(deep thud on a drum)
the flood continued for forty days,
(quiet but fast raindrops, on wood blocks, shakers, castanets, etc., playing through the next lines)
and the water became deep enough for the boat to float.
(add raindrops on chime bars and glockenspiels, etc.)
The water became deeper and the boat drifted on the surface.
(add some cymbal crashes, but not too loud)
It became so deep that it covered the highest mountains;
(all become a little louder)

MUSIC

it went on rising until it was seven metres above the tops of the mountain.
(the music swells, the cymbal crashes, the music fades and returns to quiet raindrops played slowly)
Every living thing on the earth died.
(the rain stops – there is silence)
Every bird, every animal and every person,
(quiet single drum beat, then a pause)
everything on the earth that breathed, died.
(another single drum beat)
The water did not start going down for a hundred and fifty days.
(high note droplets on glockenspiels, xylophones, chime bars, etc.)
God caused a wind to blow and the water started going down.
(droplets get lower and lower, slowing down – add a wind effect, perhaps a ssshh noise using voices)
The water kept going down, and … the tops of the mountains appeared.
(droplets eventually stop and the music ends with a gentle thud on the drum)

You may need to rehearse this piece a few times. Talk with the pupils about ways in which it could be improved. Ask questions such as "Do we really capture the right mood?" or "How can we make our picce better?" Make sure the narrators put the right expressions into their voices to help with the atmosphere.

Further work
Using other parts of the Noah story (or another story if you wish) the pupils could create further soundscapes. Always be careful to use a story that you feel lends itself well to this treatment. Pupils can perform their piece in a school assembly.

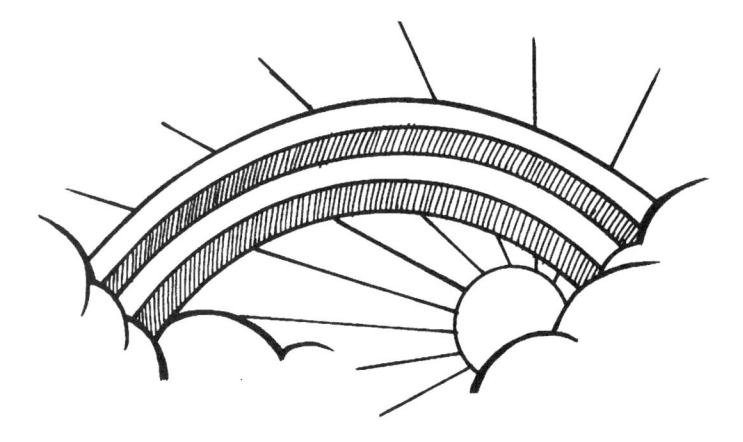

An example
Elijah and the whisper

Elijah moaning
  Two tone ▱. Scrape one side then the other, x 3

Wind
  ╱ x 2, ╰╮ x 1. Repeat

Earthquake
  Small ⊘ x 2
  Large ⊘ x 2
  Strike the note A on 🎵...

Fire
  ◯, quietly then loud

Whisper
  🎵 F A G G F A, x 2

Happiness
  🎺 for 5 seconds

Nathan Kohut and Sinead Conroy, Year 4, Albany Junior School, Stapleford

Biblical application
This technique can be used on many stories to capture the mood. The project here is setting a biblical passage to music in such a way that pupils evoke the atmosphere of the story. The story of Noah is a sombre one which ends on a note of hope which can be reflected in the music. The story of the flood needs sensitive handling and time should be allowed for discussion and talking over different issues.

Through discussion with the pupils you could refine or add further ideas. You can also transfer this way of working to other stories from the Bible and produce some original and creative compositions (see the section on the creation, page 108).

More information on choral speaking can be found on pages 118–119 of *Story and Drama*. The Dramatised Bible (Marshall Pickering/Bible Society, 1989) is the Bible arranged for this approach.

MUSIC

Soundscape (2)

Creation: Genesis 1.1—2.25
Creation poems: Psalms 8.3–4; 19.1; 104; 136.1–9; 139.13–18; 147.1, 4–9, 15–18; 148.1–10
The creator: Isaiah 40.26, 28

NOTE: Do not try this project until you have looked at "The great flood" or "Let my people go" (pages 105 and 88–90).

Read the beginning of Genesis with the pupils, and ask them to write down what God created on each of the first six days. Using the ideas in "Soundscape (1)", invent a short musical effect for each of the days.

Now join the six ideas pupils have invented to make a more extended composition called "The Creation". The sections could be joined by a narrator who reads out the appropriate words for each part. The teacher can organize this activity by arranging the class into six groups. Decide if you want an effect for the seventh day when God rested. Listen to extracts from Haydn's *Creation* – especially the beginning.

The passages from Psalms and Isaiah can be used in follow-up work or they can be the basis for "musical poems". Pupils can create musical effects for the poems.

DETAILED ACTIVITIES

An example
   Recurring music

Voice of God
   [woodblock] x 4

Days of creation
   [claves] 1 hit for first day, 2 for second, etc.

Creation story
Emptiness
   [maracas] every 4 seconds, x 4

Light
   [cymbal] crash

Space and sky
   Beater dragged over [xylophone]

Dry land and seas
   [woodblock] x 3, followed by [tambourine] x 4, (repeat sequence)

Vegetation
   [xylophone] A B C C B A A B C, x 3; add in [maracas] and crumpled paper for rustling sounds

Sun, moon, and stars
   [cymbal] crash; shake of a [tambourine]; random high notes on [xylophone]

Water animals
   [guiro] alternating with [woodblock], x 5

Birds
   Irregular notes on [guiro]; cuckoo call, x 3

Land animals
   [claves] x 5 (hoofbeats)

Man and woman
   [cymbal] x 2, [drum] x 2, [triangle] x 2, played together

Rest
   Silence

Laura Archer, Keira Welch, Matthew Doar, and Robert Beattie, Year 6, Fairfield School, Stapleford

109

MUSIC

Sad stories, sad tunes

David's lament over Jonathan: 2 Samuel 1.1–27
The widow of Nain: Luke 7.11–17
Jairus' daughter: Matthew 9.18–26; Mark 5.21–43; Luke 8.18–56

Description of the activity

For this activity, pupils listen to or read a story and decide what made the people sad. A sad song is then created using three elements – the tune, the drone and the accompaniment. Each reinforces the sadness of the story. Before pupils try this activity, they might like to listen to some sad music (page 76).

Creating a sad tune

In this project pupils compose their own sad tune and the teacher connects it with a sad story of their own choice.

For this sad tune, pupils use:

A tune (in this piece sad sounding notes are used)

A drone (a musical idea where the same notes are repeated over and over again as background to the main tune);

Some accompaniment (music which supports the tune)

The tune

Use the following rhythm (the words are just there to help people remember how the rhythm goes).

DETAILED ACTIVITIES

This is my ve-ry sad song. (wait)

Using only the notes ABC and E, pupils invent a tune to fit the rhythm. They can use recorder, chime bars, glockenspiel, keyboards, etc. When they invent their own tune, try to encourage them to move from note to note without having too many big jumps. They can repeat the same note. Here is an example:

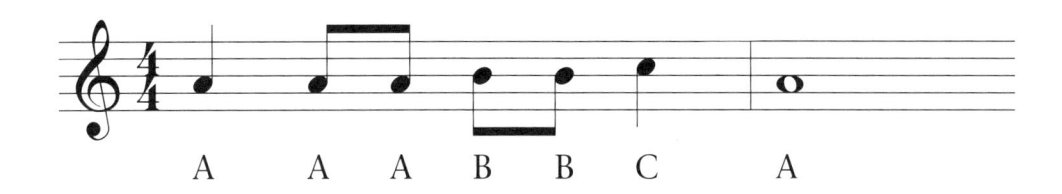

A A A B B C A

When they are satisfied with their one line of music, they can make it last longer by playing it four times. Remember, the speed will be slow to make it sad.

The drone

Have the notes A and E played low on the piano or keyboard. Play to the rhythm "sad song".

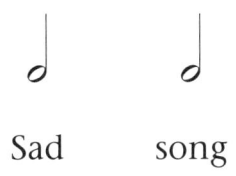

Sad   song

Play the rhythm slowly to fit with the tune. Of course, you will have to play it several times over. A drone like this adds to the sad effect.

The accompaniment

Use some small percussion instruments to add more colour. They could play the same rhythm as the drone or as the tune. They could take it in turns to play different lines.

The project might end up with a piece like this:

Line one: tune and drone play (accompanied by slow beat on tambourines)

Lines two and three: tune and drone play (accompanied by shakers playing tune rhythm)

Line four: tune and drone play (accompanied by all playing quietly)

For more variety, pupils can invent a different tune for line three – perhaps even using a new rhythm. Listen to the final performance and ask "Are we making our piece sound sad?" "What can we do to improve it?"

MUSIC

An example
Jairus' daughter, 1st part

$\frac{4}{4}$ B A A C C E | B

Tiffany Hathaway, Year 5, Albany School, Stapleford

Biblical application
There are many sad stories in the Bible and stories with a sad element. This activity can be used to express that sadness, once the story has been read and discussed. For some stories, pupils will need to combine this with the joyful tune activity which follows.

Joyful stories, joyful tunes

Deborah rejoices: Judges 5.1–11
Jairus' daughter: Matthew 9.18–26; Mark 5.21–43; Luke 8.18–56
The lame man: Acts 3.1–16

Description of the activity
This activity follows a similar pattern to the sad tune exercise on page 110. A simple tune and accompaniment combined with speed, a higher pitch of note, and faster rhythm, can produce a joyful effect. Before pupils attempt to write their own joyful tune they should listen to some joyful music (page 76). How does it make them feel?
What does it make them want to do?
What speed is the music?
Is it high or low?

Ask the pupils to clap or tap on a drum a joyful rhythm. This rhythm is based on Calypso.

Create a simple tune to this rhythm using only the notes C E G and A. These can be played on the recorder, piano, keyboard, chime bars, or glockenspiel. Any note can be used more than once.

Pupils can add musical accompaniment to their tune. Discuss which instruments they would choose and how they might be played. The accompaniment can join in progressively, adding to the joyful effect, rather than joining in all at once.

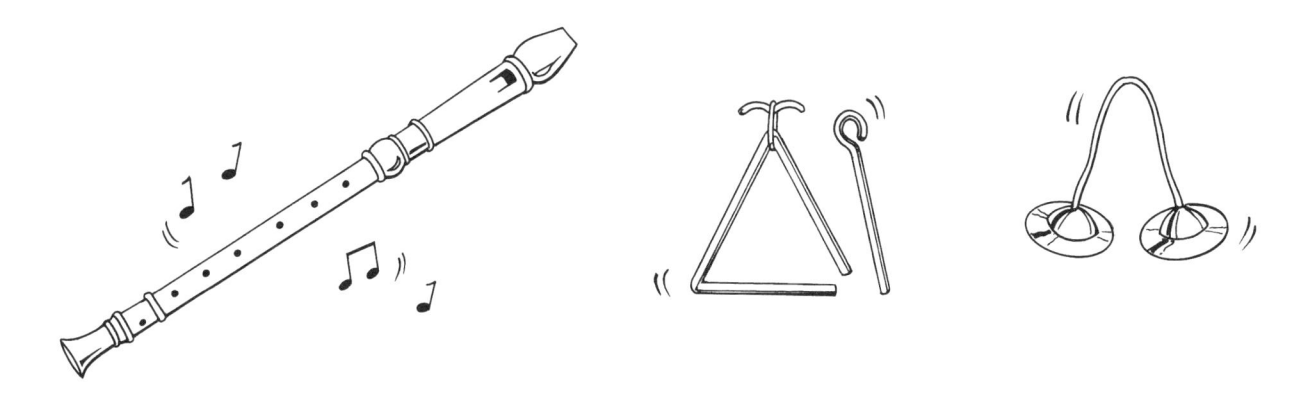

An example
Jairus' daughter, 2nd part

C E G A G E G A C   C E G A G E G A C

Matthew Baillon, Year 5, Albany School, Stapleford

Biblical application
Talk about the things which make people joyful. Read a Bible story such as the lame man and discuss what created the joy on this occasion. For stories such as Jairus' daughter, both sad and joyful tunes can be used.

MUSIC

Musical characters

Martha and Mary: Luke 11.38–42
The good Samaritan: Luke 10.25–37
The Pharisee and the tax collector: Luke 18.9–14

Description of the activity

Play the piece "Peter and the Wolf" by Prokofiev to the pupils. Ask them to listen to the way each character in the story has their own tune. Pupils can create their own tunes for characters from a story. The role and personality of the characters should be discussed and the results of these discussions should be expressed in the tunes produced.

The good Samaritan

In the story of the good Samaritan, there are a number of characters. For this piece, pupils will need a tune or musical effect for each of them. Their tune should represent the kind of person they are. This list will help pupils invent their tunes.

The man (a Jew) – a simple effect at walking speed;

The robbers – a loud, violent effect;

The burning sun – a "hot" pulse;

The priest – a noble, aloof tune;

The Levite – a nervous tune;

The good Samaritan – an effect to suggest compassion, perhaps a hymn tune played quietly;

The innkeeper – a jolly effect.

Pupils can, of course, use their own ideas for their characters.
They could try miming the story and illustrating it with the appropriate tunes or effects.
At times this might mean playing some tunes or effects together.

An example
The good Samaritan

Footsteps
 🧱 x 10, getting louder

Attack
 🎵 x 5, 🥁 x 10, loudly

Hot sun
 🔔 hit with metal x 10, △ x 10, alternating

Priest
 🎹 F F A G B C F, as he approaches;
he runs away: 🧱 x 20, getting faster

Levite
 Repeat as for priest

Traveller's despair
 🎹 C C D D, x 5, played together in pairs

Donkey
 🧱 x 16, getting louder

Helping
 🎹 GFGG, x 2, quietly

At the inn
 🎹 padded hammers gliding up and down

Paul Johnson and Abby Rischer, Year 5, Christopher McLaughlin and Kimberly Dinan, Year 6, St John's Church of England School, Stapleford

MUSIC

Biblical application
This technique can be used on any biblical story with two or more characters with very different personalities. In the case of Mary and Martha, although sisters, they are opposites in personality. The Pharisee and the tax collector would need very different tunes, one to express pride, the other repentance.

Chant

The coming of Jesus: Isaiah 2.14; 9.6–7; 11.6–9

Description of the activity
Gregorian chant (or plain chant or plainsong) is the body of ancient melodies still used in the Roman Catholic Church (now often sung in translation from the original Latin). It developed very early in Church history, arising from the cantor's role in the Jewish synagogue, and uses the rhythms of human speech, being non-rhyming and irregular.

From simple beginnings with a single melody line sung by the congregation unaccompanied, chant gradually became very elaborate and complicated, needing a choir for its performance. This development was achieved for two reasons: to represent God's glory to the people, and to reflect the Church's growing political importance. At first, the melodies were handed down orally. The invention of notation (the means of recording melody as written notes, then on a 4- not 5-line stave) enabled this further elaboration. Various movements have sought to restore chant's original simplicity.

O come, O come, Immanuel
This tune has developed through the years from an original chant melody. It needs to be sung, preferably unaccompanied, and very simply, to reflect its origins. The words refer to the Christian belief that Jesus, who came once as a baby in Bethlehem, will return as King of the world. (They are a translation of a Latin hymn from the thirteenth century).

O Come, O Come Immanuel

From the Great O Antiphons (12th–13th centuries)
Translated by John Mason Neale (1818–66)   Melody adapted by Thomas Helmore

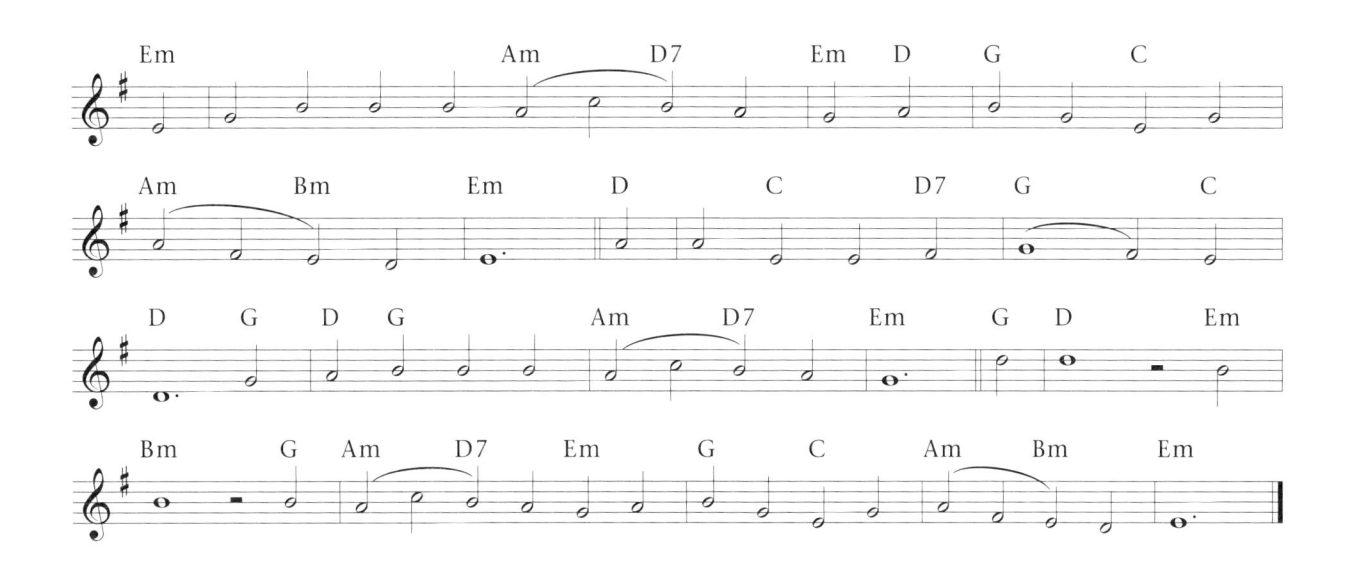

1. O come, O come, Immanuel
And ransom captive Israel.
That mourns in lonely exile here,
Until the Son of God appear.
Rejoice rejoice! Immanuel
Shall come to thee, O Israel.

2. O come, O come, Thou Lord of might
Who to Thy tribes on Sinai's height,
In ancient times didst give the law
In cloud and majesty and awe;
Rejoice, rejoice, etc.

3. O come, Thou Rod of Jesse, free
Thine own from Satan's tyranny;
From depths of hell thy people save,
And give them victory o'er the grave:
Rejoice, rejoice, etc.

4. O come, Thou Dayspring, come and cheer
Our spirits by Thine advent here;
Disperse the gloomy clouds of night,
And death's dark shadows put to flight:
Rejoice, rejoice, etc.

5. O come, Thou Key of David, come
And open wide our heavenly home;
Make safe the way that leads on high
And close the path to misery:
Rejoice, rejoice, etc.

MUSIC

Talk about processions with the children. Discuss the different types of processions: funerals, weddings, carnivals, etc. Some are happy, some are sad occasions. Listen to this music. If this was a procession, how would the people be walking? How would they look?

An example

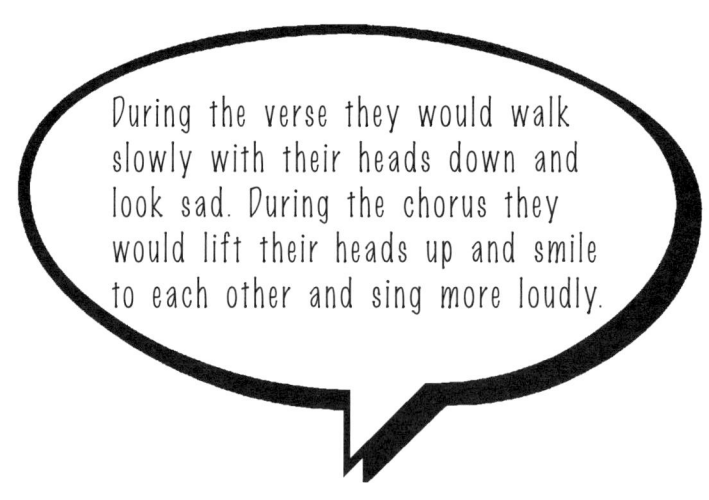

> During the verse they would walk slowly with their heads down and look sad. During the chorus they would lift their heads up and smile to each other and sing more loudly.

Pupils of Albany Junior School, Stapleford

Biblical application

This chant can be used with the Christmas story, or as part of the celebration of Advent looking at the prophecies concerning Jesus. Christians believe God kept his promises made in those prophecies. Explain the background of the music to pupils and read out the words. This chant is still sung before Christmas. It reflects Christians' longing for Jesus to come to our world full of wrong. It also has a note of rejoicing, for Christians remember that Jesus did come with his message of peace and love at Christmas.

Carols

The Christmas story: Matthew 1.18–25; 2.1–12; Luke 1.26–28; 2.1–20
The rejection at Nazareth: Luke 4.14–28

Description of the activity

Carols were originally circular dances which were popular in mediaeval Europe. "Carol" as a title was then transferred to the songs which were sung to these dances. Initially they were not religious songs; in fact the Church opposed their use because they were secular dance tunes. When they were finally accepted in church the carols were sung by choirs, not danced. The early carols used in worship were, elsewhere, often danced in procession. The carol started with the chorus which was danced. People rested during the verse.

DETAILED ACTIVITIES

There has been some debate about how much they were danced in processions. Some think the people walked during the chorus and stood still for the verses. However, ordinary people probably danced them outside formal church worship: they were a joyous expression of popular faith. Many are written in dance rhythms or make you want to dance. Listen to the Sussex Carol (On Christmas night all Christians sing).

Saint Francis of Assisi was one of the first to introduce lively tunes into Christmas worship. He set up a nativity tableau in a cave in Greccio in Italy and invited people to come to see the scene. Some of the monks wrote music for the worship, which was held around the crib, using joyous tunes which were more like carols.

Carols were particularly popular at Christmas, and eventually the term was applied to any religious Christmas song, though carols were written for many other occasions.

The early carols were not written down: they were linked to simple melodies which varied from region to region and were similar to folk songs. "Nova, nova" is an example of an early carol, with the chorus at the beginning, it has a lively dance-like rhythm. Groups of children could design a dance to perform during the chorus.

The Latin *Nova, nova* could be translated "Good news, good news". The next words, *Ave fit ex Eva* mean "Greetings to you who are descended from Eve". The *"nova"* could also be a play on words, likening Mary to a new Eve (Eva). Just as eternal life was lost by Eve this "new Eve" will give birth to the person who will give others eternal life. The final words are Mary's answer to the angel: "Behold, the servant of the Lord," in Luke 1.38.

MUSIC

Nova, nova

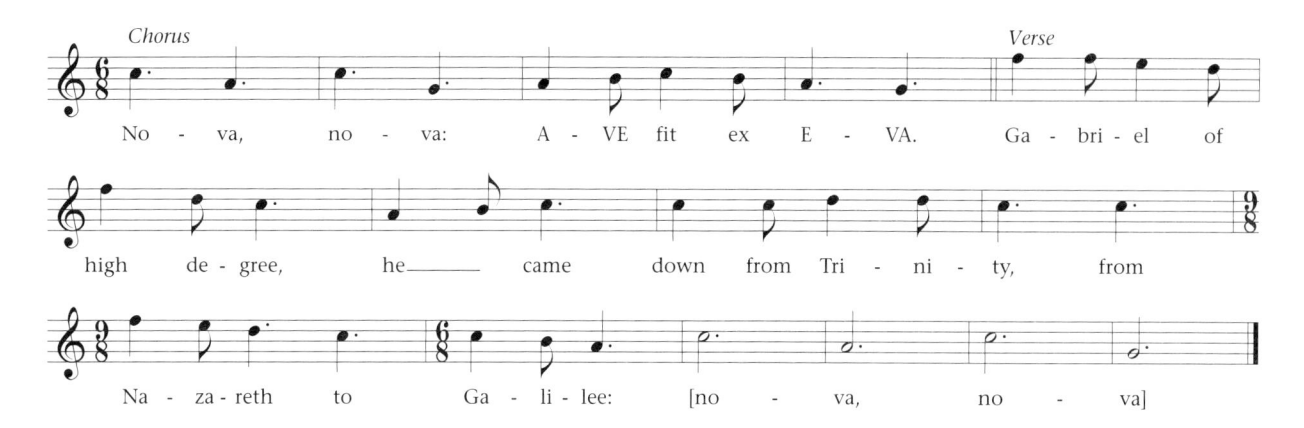

[Musical notation: Chorus and Verse in 6/8 time]

No-va, no-va: A-VE fit ex E-VA. Ga-bri-el of high de-gree, he—— came down from Tri-ni-ty, from Na-za-reth to Ga-li-lee: [no-va, no-va]

2. I met a maiden in a place;
I kneeled down afore her face
And said: Hail, Mary, full of grace;

3. When the maiden heard tell of this,
She was full sore abashed y–wis,
And weened that she had done amiss;

4. Then said the angel; Dread not thou,
For ye be conceived with great virtue
Whose name shall be called Jesu;

5. It is not yet six weeks agone
Sin Elizabeth conceived John,
As it was prophesied beforn;

6. Then said the maiden: Verily,
I am your servant right truly;
Ecce, ancilla Domini.

Pupils can create a ring dance for this carol that will express its mood. They need to listen to the music first and decide whether it is happy, sad, etc. Pupils should record their dance so that it can be danced "from the page".

An example
(1) link hands and hold them up
(2) skip round to the left for the chorus
(3) on the next chorus point left foot forward then back, then drop hands and skip in individual circles.

Nathan Kohut and Sinead Conroy, Albany Junior School, Stapleford

Biblical application

Carols are a joyous celebration. The whole of Jesus' life was described by the term "gospel" – good news. Pupils can look through the Christmas story and decide what was good news about it, then look at Jesus' job description in Luke 4.

Psalms

Praise of God: Psalms 47; 136

Description of the activity

The psalms are the Hebrew poems of the Book of Psalms in the Old Testament, written by David and others. They were an integral part of Jewish worship in the Temple, sung by the Levites. Adapting this practice, the earliest Christians sang the psalms, in Latin or Greek, in their own services. There are two main ways of singing the psalms, both still a part of Roman Catholic worship.

> Responsorial Psalms. In these the congregation responds to the priest. The priest would sing a line from a psalm and the congregation responds by singing back.

> Antiphons. Originally an antiphon was a refrain between verses, but soon the antiphon developed to stand by itself as a worship song.

At the Reformation, the growing Protestant churches laid great emphasis on worship being in the people's own language. The psalms were therefore translated into many languages. These rhymed, metrical (with a regular metre) translations were collected into books called psalters. The psalms were now presented in the light of New Testament teaching, especially by the Calvinists and by Isaac Watts, who published a very influential collection.

Hymns, which were not as entirely biblical as the psalms, were beginning to be popular with the Protestants. But the Church of England used only psalms for many more years. During the Commonwealth, under Oliver Cromwell, in fact, people were allowed to sing only psalms. Afterwards, there was a great explosion of hymn writing and psalms became less dominant in Anglican worship.

MUSIC

Psalm 47

From one of the best known metrical psalters of the seventeenth century, this is a free translation – a paraphrase of Psalm 47.

Psalm 47

Tune from Ravenscroft's seventeenth-century psalter

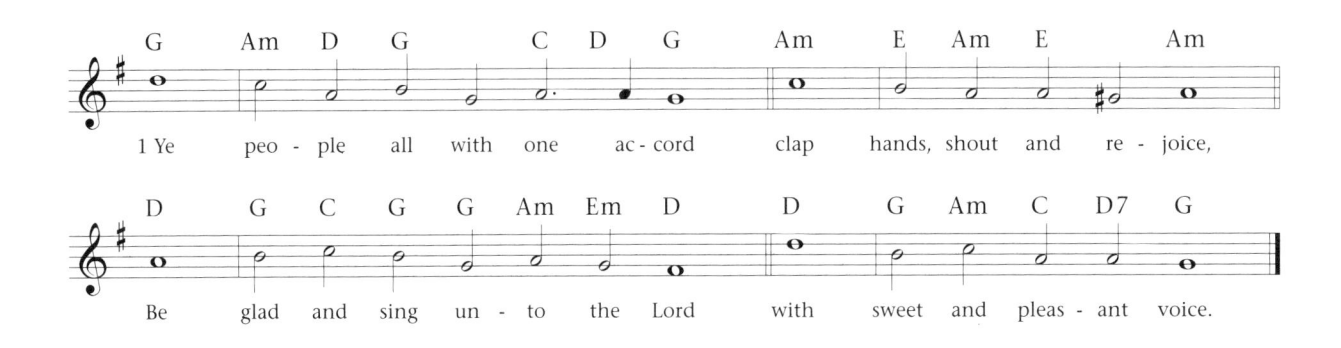

[Musical notation with chords G, Am, D, G, C, D, G, Am, E, Am, E, Am above the lyrics:]

1 Ye peo-ple all with one ac-cord clap hands, shout and re-joice,

[Second line with chords D, G, C, G, G, Am, Em, D, D, G, Am, C, D7, G:]

Be glad and sing un-to the Lord with sweet and pleas-ant voice.

Discuss how we associate different types of music with different places. Some people think that church music ought to be slow and quiet. Puritan psalms were sung by people who thought music should be simple, not distract from the words, and be suitable for praising God. Their whole lifestyle was one of simplicity. Look at puritan clothes and churches. Can you see a link between the music and puritan lifestyle in general?

An example

> Everything they did seems to be plain simple but clear and perfect.

Pupils of George Spencer School, Stapleford

DETAILED ACTIVITIES

Biblical application

The psalms are the songs of the Bible. The words of the Bible were very important to the puritans. Some puritan musicians only wrote one beat for each syllable (as in this case) so that words were not muddled or distorted. Pupils can look at other biblical psalms which are still sung, such as "Let us with a gladsome mind" (Psalm 136).

Hymns

The lost sheep: Luke 15.1–7
The man born blind: John 9

Description of the activity

A hymn is a song of praise to God. It consists of several verses, occasionally with a chorus, using the same structure and tune in each verse.

Hymns grew out of psalms. In New Testament times and up to the fifth century, they were paraphrases of biblical passages. But then their composition became freer. They took on a teaching purpose, adding New Testament teaching to their content, and introduced personal experience. We still have Latin hymn books from the eleventh and twelfth centuries.

At the Reformation, the emerging Protestant churches laid great importance on the use of the congregations' own language in services. The Lutherans used contemporary popular tunes and new compositions for their new hymns. The Calvanists preferred adaptations of the old psalm tunes. In England, in 1719, Isaac Watts published his Psalter containing modernized versions of the psalms, but still using the former psalms' strict metrical forms. But, with the Evangelical Revival of the 1730s, the English hymn as we know it took form. The Wesleys, Toplady, Whitefield and Newton all produced many hymns, original in content and in tune, in a wide variety of metrical forms, based on personal experience, and seeking to present the Christian message as simply as possible. These were very popular with Nonconformists in England, and, eventually, in America. But the Church of England officially did not have its own hymn book until the mid-nineteenth century. In some churches in Scotland, the older forms and methods of singing still thrive today.

Victorian hymn writers were very prolific and earlier traditions almost disappeared in these years. America's gospel hymns and spirituals have also influenced English hymn writers.

MUSIC

Amazing Grace

This hymn was written by John Newton, a former slave trader who fought to abolish the trade. It is based on his personal experience, comparing his former life to his present one as a Christian. It contains references to incidents in the Bible: for instance:

"lost and found" – the sheep in Luke 15.1–7;

"blind and see" – the healed blind man in John 9.

It could be accompanied by a piano or keyboard. Some children could develop a dance to accompany it, using mime.

Amazing Grace Virginia Harmony 1831
John Newton Arranged for guitar by S Hatherly

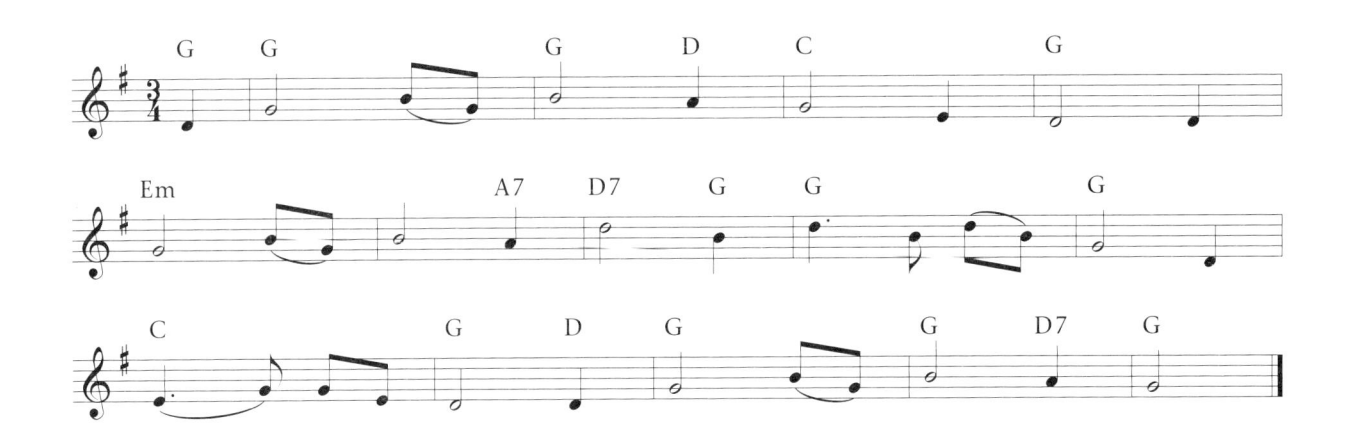

1. Amazing grace! how sweet the sound
That saves a wretch like me!
I once was lost but now am found;
Was blind but now I see.

2. 'Twas grace that taught my heart
   to fear,
And grace my fears relieved
How precious did that grace appear
The hour I first believed!

3. Through many dangers, toils and snares
I have already come;
'Tis grace has brought me safe thus far,
And grace will lead me home.

4. The Lord has promised good to me,
His Word my hopes secures;
He will my shield and portion be
As long as life endures.

5. Yes, when this flesh and heart shall fail,
And mortal life shall cease,
I shall possess within the veil
A life of joy and peace.

6. When I've been there a thousand years,
Bright shining as the sun,
I've no less days to sing God's praise
Than when I first begun.

Talk about the life of John Newton. Ask children what they think the words of "Amazing grace" tell about Newton's life and character. He was lost to goodness and God. He was blind to cruelty and wrong.

An example

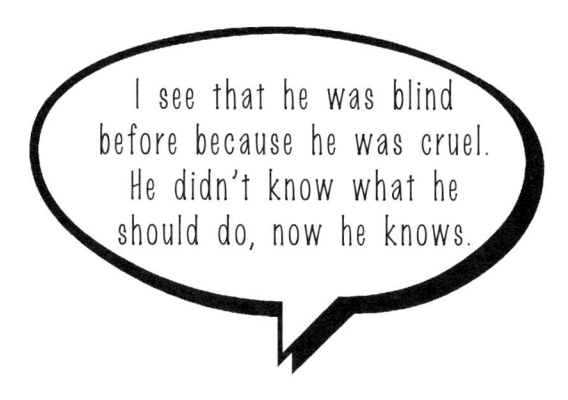

> I see that he was blind before because he was cruel. He didn't know what he should do, now he knows.

Matthew Baillon and Tiffany Hathaway, Year 5, Albany Junior School, Stapleford

Biblical application
Music sometimes arises out of specific situations. Many hymns reflect personal experiences in this way. The writers of the hymns were steeped in the Bible, and when they write about their own experiences they often use the words of the Bible, as Newton does referring to two biblical stories. Look at the hymn "I heard the voice of Jesus say" and use the references Matthew 11.25–30; John 4.13 and 9.5.

Spirituals

The fall of Jericho: Joshua 5—6

Description of the activity
Spirituals are a type of religious folk song, developed by the African slaves brought to America during the time of the slave trade. They brought a strong musical tradition with them, which can be traced in the spirituals. West African music used complicated rhythms, syncopation (where the stress falls off the beat) and a frequent use of a five-note scale. (We use an eight-note scale). Other influences on the spiritual included the Bible and Gospel songs heard from travelling evangelists at the Camp Meetings which were popular at the time.

Often, spirituals have a call-and-response format, reminiscent of the slaves "field hollers" and work songs. They have a simple melody, but a complex rhythm using syncopation. The theme is nearly always future freedom: the slaves looked forward to their coming freedom in heaven, and to the hoped-for earthly freedom. But even after emancipation, the black people of the South suffered greatly under the new segregation laws. So the theme of longing for a release from present suffering continued.

Spirituals first came to a wider audience when the Fisk Jubilee Singers (followed by other groups) began touring America to raise money for a university for black people – although there is a disagreement about the degree of accuracy with which their white manager allowed them to sing the spirituals.

Spirituals have had a widespread influence on such composers as Stephen Foster and George Gershwin, and in musical genres such as jazz, blues, rhythm and blues, and soul. The tradition of gospel singing still thrives in black churches.

Joshua fit the Battle of Jericho

This is a simplified version of a well-known spiritual describing Joshua's defeat of the city of Jericho, found in the Book of Joshua, chapters 5 and 6. It was a popular theme as it showed the triumph of God's people over great adversity, through obedience to God's commands. Many spirituals are solemn, reflecting the slaves' sorrow and longing, but this one is triumphant.

It should be sung in a lively, swinging rhythm, with a triumphant air. An appropriate accompaniment would be clapping in rhythm, or the use of percussion instruments to stress the beat.

DETAILED ACTIVITIES

Joshua fit the battle of Jericho

2. Up to the walls of Jericho
He marched with spear in hand.
"Go blow them ram-horns," Joshua cried,
"Cause the battle am in my hand."

*Joshua fit the battle of Jericho, Jericho, Jericho,
Joshua fit the battle of Jericho,
And the walls came tumbling down.*

3. Then the ram-sheep's horns began to blow,
Trumpets began to sound.
Joshua commanded the children to shout,
And the walls came tumbling down,
    that morning

MUSIC

A spiritual which shows the longing for freedom, "Let my people go", can be found on page 89.

This is based on the story found in Exodus 3—11, in which Moses repeatedly asks Pharaoh to release the Israelite slaves from Egypt. The biblical account culminated in their release, so its appeal to the slaves is easy to understand. It should be sung to reflect the slave's sorrow in their situation, and their great longing for freedom.

Talk about spirituals with pupils. Why did the slaves sing about characters such as Moses and Joshua? What other characters would be suitable material for spirituals? Why?

An example

> Daniel would be good as he was saved from the lions and the slaves needed saving from slavery. You could use David as he defeated Goliath that would encourage the slaves.

Pupils of George Spencer School, Stapleford

Biblical application

Although the Bible stories are often specific to a particular situation, the sufferings and triumphs of certain characters have come to reflect those experiences for people in general. Pupils can take a biblical story and describe how the characters' experiences would be relevant to oppressed people.

Jazz

Heaven: Revelation 21.1–5

Description of the activity

This is a style of music emerging around 1900 in New Orleans in the southern states of North America. Its origins are complicated. It took its improvisation (in which the musicians make up the tune as they play) and its use of "blue" notes (notes pitched between two notes – for example, between the B and C on a piano) from the style of the "blues" singers, who had emerged as popular singers by then. It took its syncopated rhythm (in which the "beat" or stress falls unexpectedly) from ragtime, a form of dance music, usually played on the piano. Other ingredients included black folk forms such as spirituals and work songs, which also influenced "blues"; marching bands; and the minstrel shows, which were the white version of black folk music. Soon, jazz's centre moved from New Orleans to Chicago and New York, and its popularity spread. The jazz bands grew bigger, improvisation became less possible, and the music began to be written down – originally the jazz players played by ear. The "big bands" provided "swing" – a popular dance music. Various branches of jazz since then have sought to re-establish its spontaneity and improvisation. Overshadowed by rock for a while, it is still thriving.

Usually, jazz consists of a basic tune, played repeatedly with (improvised or written) variations – played by solo instruments in the jazz band, or sung in "blues" style.

MUSIC

Oh when the Saints
Traditional   Music traditional

1. Oh when the Saints go marching in,
Oh when the Saints go marching in
I want to be in that number,
When the Saints go marching in.

2. Oh when they gather round the throne,
Oh when they gather round the throne
I want to be in that number,
When they gather round the throne.

3. Oh when the drums begin to play,
Oh when the drums begin to play
I want to be in that number,
When the drums begin to play.

4. Oh when they crown Him Lord of all,
Oh when they crown Him Lord of all
I want to be in that number,
When they crown Him Lord of all.

"When the Saints go marching in" is based on the Book of Revelation and a passage in Philippians in the Bible, describing the Christians' hope that they will be part of the "new heaven", when all sorrows will be over. This basic tune would have been sung, and then repeated with variations. This is, obviously, difficult to reconstruct! The singing should be lively, and the rhythm sharp. There are opportunities for the accompaniment to be "improvised"! Children can be encouraged to compose their own rhythmic accompaniments on simple percussion instruments, or on xylophones.

DETAILED ACTIVITIES

Play or sing the song until pupils are familiar with it. Do they want to dance when they hear music like this? Which instruments would suit the mood of this music? Pupils can experiment to find the sound that they want and how they would use it to accompany the music. They do not have to play on every note or beat.

An example

1) FACA FACA
2) C F   C F

(T = tap, S = shake)

3) TTTT   TTTT   TTTT
4) S S   S S   S S

Playing
1) Just piano plays
2) piano plus 1 and 2
3) piano plus 3 and 4
4) piano plus 1 and 3

Matthew Baillon and Tiffany Hathaway, Year 5, Albany School, Stapleford

Biblical application

The passage in Revelation is a vision of heaven: a place without tears, a place where God is. What other types of music would reflect these joyous ideas?

STORY INDEX

The initials used below refer to the volume of Toolkit in which the story concerned occurs; *WP Writing and Poetry, SD Story and Drama, AM Art and Music.*

Abraham
   and Isaac *WP* 50; *WP* 122; *AM* 59
   and God's promise *WP* 115
   leaves home *WP* 77; *WP* 126; *SD* 122

Adam and Eve *SD* 108; *SD* 126; *AM* 24

Ananias *SD* 53

anger *WP* 112; *AM* 36

annunciation *SD* 56; *SD* 126; *AM* 37; *AM* 42; *AM* 62; *AM* 118

apostles (*see* disciples)

apocalyptic writers *WP* 24

arrest of Jesus *WP* 44

ascension *AM* 40

"Ask, seek, knock" *WP* 50; *AM* 57

Baptism of Jesus *WP* 42; *WP* 131
   (*and see* John the Baptist)

Bartimaeus *WP* 122; *AM* 123

belief *WP* 101

bones, valley of dry *SD* 102

bread of life *WP* 117

bridesmaids, ten *WP* 47; *SD* 61; *SD* 67; *SD* 105

bush, burning *WP* 105

Caesar's tax *SD* 117

Cain and Abel *SD* 117

centurion's servant *SD* 42

children and Jesus *SD* 108; *SD* 113

Christmas *WP* 12; *WP* 14; *WP* 16; *WP* 40; *WP* 55; *WP* 94; *WP* 97; *WP* 127; *SD* 43; *SD* 57; *SD* 126; *AM* 24; *AM* 34; *AM* 42; *AM* 59; *AM* 62; *AM* 116; *AM* 118
   (*and see* Jesus)

coin, lost *WP* 47; *WP* 67; *WP* 119; *SD* 79; *SD* 105

"Come to me" *SD* 102

Commandments, Ten *WP* 72; *WP* 77; *SD* 42; *AM* 39; *AM* 45

creation *WP* 30; *WP* 93; *WP* 99; *WP* 107; *WP* 110; *SD* 64; *SD* 91; *SD* 108; *AM* 35; *AM* 60; *AM* 95; *AM* 108

crossing the Red Sea
   (*see* Moses)

crucifixion (*see* Jesus)

Daniel
   and the fiery furnace *SD* 70; *AM* 40; *AM* 58
   and the food *WP* 34; *SD* 47
   and the lions *WP* 69; *SD* 113
   and the writing on the wall *SD* 93; *SD* 113; *AM* 24; *AM* 42

David *WP* 29; *SD* 71; *AM* 54
   and the ark *SD* 34; *AM* 78
   and Bathsheba *SD* 95
   and Goliath *WP* 126; *SD* 34; *SD* 38; *SD* 47; *SD* 71
   and Jonathan *WP* 57; *AM* 110
   and Saul *WP* 126; *SD* 53; *SD* 104; *SD* 107
   choice of *WP* 63; *WP* 129; *SD* 38; *SD* 58
   in hiding *WP* 39

Deborah *WP* 29; *AM* 112

debtors, two *WP* 10; *WP* 27; *WP* 47

deceit *WP* 112

Delilah *SD* 69; *SD* 97

disciples *AM* 26; *AM* 95; *AM* 100
   calling of *SD* 109; *AM* 35

Dorcas *AM* 53

Easter (*see* Jesus)

Ecclesiastes *SD* 78

Elijah
   and the priests of Baal *WP* 117; *SD* 67; *AM* 41; *AM* 76; *AM* 85

133

ART AND MUSIC TOOLKIT

and the ravens *WP* 36; *AM* 56
and the still small voice *WP* 65; *AM* 76
and the widow *WP* 36
death of *SD* 116; *AM* 38

Elisha
and the Syrians *SD* 110
and the widow's oil *SD* 46
and the woman of Shunem's son *AM* 53

Eli's sons *SD* 109

entry into Jerusalem *WP* 44; *WP* 60; *SD* 98; *AM* 83

envy *WP* 112; *AM* 36

Ephesus *WP* 69; *SD* 52

Esau *WP* 32; *WP* 70; *WP* 115; *SD* 97; *SD* 123

Esther *WP* 70; *SD* 37; *SD* 70; *AM* 55; *AM* 62

evil speech *WP* 112; *AM* 36

Exodus (*see* **Moses**)

Ezekiel *SD* 102

Ezra *WP* 25

fear *WP* 112; *AM* 36

feast, great *SD* 60; *SD* 100; *AM* 59

feeding of the five thousand *WP* 42; *SD* 67; *AM* 50; *AM* 98

flight into Egypt *WP* 77; *SD* 122; *AM* 92

fool, rich *WP* 47; *SD* 60

forgiveness *WP* 10

friend at midnight *WP* 47; *SD* 105

furnace, fiery *SD* 71; *AM* 40; *AM* 58

garden of Gethsemane *AM* 41

gate, "I am the…" *WP* 117

Gideon *WP* 31; *SD* 100; *AM* 86
choice of *SD* 58

giving and generosity *WP* 52; *WP* 60; *WP* 119

gratitude *WP* 100

God
as a fortress *AM* 52
as shepherd *AM* 51

God's care *WP* 96

Goliath (*see* **David**)

gospel *WP* 26

hand, the man with a withered *WP* 31; *WP* 120

Hannah *SD* 47; *SD* 104

harvest *WP* 13; *AM* 37

Heaven *AM* 129

history *WP* 25

Holy Spirit *WP* 13
(*and see* **Pentecost**)

honesty *WP* 52

houses, the two *WP* 47; *SD* 42; *SD* 44

"I am" sayings *WP* 117; *AM* 35

Isaac
and Abraham *WP* 50; *WP* 122
birth of *AM* 59
(*and see* **Jacob**)

Jacob
cheats Esau *WP* 32; *WP* 70; *SD* 97
meets Esau *SD* 123
meets Rachel *WP* 60
tricks Isaac *WP* 32; *WP* 70

Jairus' daughter *WP* 74; *SD* 70; *AM* 53; *AM* 110; *AM* 112

jealousy *WP* 112; *AM* 36

Jeremiah
and the scroll *SD* 39
calling of *SD* 58
in the pit *WP* 65; *WP* 105; *SD* 98
life of *AM* 49

Jericho *AM* 95; *AM* 125

Jesus *WP* 77
and children *SD* 108; *SD* 113
and the money-changers *WP* 32; *WP* 47; *WP* 114
arrest of *WP* 44
ascension of *AM* 40
as a child *WP* 61; *WP* 74; *SD* 43; *SD* 110
as a criminal *WP* 74
as a friend *WP* 61; *WP* 74
as a miracle worker *WP* 61; *WP* 74

INDEX

as a storyteller *WP* 61; *WP* 74
as a teacher *WP* 57; *WP* 61; *SD* 99; *SD* 102; *SD* 110; *SD* 124
baptism of *WP* 42; *WP* 131
betrayal of *WP* 129; *AM* 55
birth of *WP* 11; *WP* 14; *WP* 16; *WP* 40; *WP* 55; *WP* 94; *WP* 97; *WP* 127; *SD* 43; *SD* 56; *SD* 126; *AM* 24; *AM* 37; *AM* 42; *AM* 62; *AM* 116; *AM* 118
calls the disciples *SD* 109
death of *WP* 131; *SD* 117; *AM* 37; *AM* 41; *AM* 58; *AM* 65
entry into Jerusalem *WP* 44; *WP* 60; *WP* 119; *SD* 96; *SD* 98; *AM* 73; *AM* 83
feet washed *WP* 70
flight into Egypt *WP* 77; *SD* 122
garden of Gethsemane *SD* 35; *AM* 26; *AM* 41
"I am" sayings *WP* 117; *AM* 35
Last Supper (*and see* death of) *WP* 67
rejected at Nazareth *SD* 43; *AM* 118
resurrection *WP* 40; *WP* 105; *WP* 131; *SD* 97; *SD* 128; *AM* 37; *AM* 53; *AM* 59; *AM* 65; *AM* 82
temptation *AM* 41
transfiguration *WP* 42; *WP* 110; *AM* 40
trial before Pilate (*and see* death of) *WP* 74
walks on water *AM* 45
(*and see* **disciples, John the Baptist, miracles, parables, prayer, sermon on the mount, teachings of Jesus, Temple**

Job *WP* 23; *WP* 122; *AM* 33

John the Baptist
baptism of Jesus *WP* 42; *WP* 131
birth of *WP* 63
death of *WP* 44; *WP* 131
teaching of *WP* 63; *WP* 93; *WP* 131

Jonah *WP* 77; *WP* 94; *WP* 129; *SD* 64; *AM* 38; *AM* 50; *AM* 58; *AM* 76

Jonathan *WP* 57; *AM* 110

Joseph *WP* 29; *WP* 74; *SD* 37; *SD* 61; *SD* 70; *AM* 54; *AM* 55; *AM* 100
and his brothers *SD* 107
and Pharaoh's dreams *SD* 44
as a boy *WP* 127
as a slave *WP* 120

Joshua *WP* 114
and Jericho *WP* 114; *SD* 80; *SD* 95; *SD* 125
as a spy *SD* 110

Judas *WP* 129; *AM* 55

kind words *WP* 112; *AM* 36

Law *WP* 25; *WP* 72
(*and see* **Commandments**)

Lazarus *AM* 53; *AM* 83

Leah *WP* 129

lepers, ten *WP* 127; *AM* 49

letters *WP* 23

light of the world, "I am the…" *WP* 117

lions (*see* **Daniel**)

love *WP* 57; *WP* 101; *WP* 112; *WP* 124

man at the gate *SD* 104; *SD* 123; *AM* 54; *AM* 112

man born blind *SD* 117; *AM* 123

man let down through the roof *SD* 46

man with a withered hand *WP* 31; *WP* 120

Martha and Mary *WP* 32; *WP* 74; *SD* 63; *AM* 114

Mary Magdalene *WP* 105; *SD* 97
(*and see* **resurrection**)

mind *AM* 57

miracles
Bartimaeus *WP* 122; *AM* 123
centurion's servant *SD* 42
feeding the five thousand *WP* 42; *SD* 67; *AM* 50; *AM* 98
Jairus' daughter *WP* 74; *SD* 70; *AM* 53; *AM* 110; *AM* 112
Lazarus *WP* 53; *AM* 83
lepers, ten *WP* 127; *AM* 49
man born blind *SD* 117; *AM* 123
man let down through the roof *SD* 46
man with a withered hand *WP* 31; *WP* 120
stilling the storm *WP* 65; *WP* 119; *AM* 64
walking on water *AM* 45
wedding at Cana *WP* 34; *SD* 39; *SD* 46
widow of Nain's son *AM* 83; *AM* 110
woman bent double *WP* 34; *WP* 61
woman with a haemorrhage *WP* 115; *SD* 99

money-changers *WP* 44; *WP* 114

Moses *WP 29; WP 61*
   in the bulrushes *WP 96; SD 39*
   and the burning bush *WP 105*
   Exodus, including crossing the Red Sea and the escape from Egypt *WP 44; WP 77; WP 107; SD 122; AM 64; AM 88*
   manna and quail *WP 77; AM 92*
   plagues of Egypt *SD 100; AM 49; AM 88*
   Ten Commandments *WP 72; WP 77; SD 42; AM 39; AM 45; AM 92*

Naaman *WP 55; SD 66*

Naboth's Vineyard *WP 40; SD 95*

Naomi *WP 11; WP 57; WP 124; SD 63; SD 95; AM 54*

Nehemiah *WP 39*

Noah *SD 116; AM 41; AM 65; AM 105*

Parable *WP 27*

Parables told by Jesus
   friend at midnight *WP 47; SD 105*
   good Samaritan *WP 47; WP 55; WP 77; WP 110; WP 119; SD 60; SD 98; AM 88; AM 114*
   great feast *SD 60; SD 100; AM 59*
   lost coin *WP 47; WP 67; WP 119; SD 79; SD 105*
   lost sheep *WP 47; WP 59; SD 64; AM 49; AM 123*
   lost son (prodigal son) *WP 39; WP 47; WP 55; SD 94; AM 59*
   pearl *WP 47*
   Pharisee and tax collector *WP 72; SD 52; AM 114,*
   prodigal son (*see* lost son)
   rich fool *WP 47; SD 60*
   rich man and Lazarus *SD 63*
   sheep and goats *WP 47; SD 38; SD 47; SD 60*
   sower *WP 36; WP 47; WP 72; SD 60; SD 66; SD 107*
   talents *WP 47; WP 69*
   ten bridesmaids *WP 47; SD 61; SD 67; SD 105*
   treasure *WP 47*
   two builders (*see* two houses)
   two debtors *WP 10; WP 27; WP 47*
   two houses *WP 47; SD 42; SD 44*
   two sons *WP 31*
   unforgiving servant *WP 59; SD 38; SD 69*
   weeds *AM 60*
   workers in the vineyard *SD 61; SD 69*

Paul *WP 61; SD 37*
   and Philemon *WP 23; SD 83*
   at Ephesus *WP 69; SD 52*
   conversion of *SD 53; SD 71; SD 12; AM 45*
   letters of *AM 57*

peace *WP 112; AM 36*

pearl *WP 47*

Pentecost *WP 13; WP 107; SD 107; SD 116; AM 37; AM 59; AM 62*
   (*and see* **Holy Spirit**)

Peter *WP 61*
   confesses Christ *WP 124*
   denies Jesus *SD 53; SD 108*
   heals lame man at gate *SD 104; SD 123*
   Sapphira and Ananias *WP 44*
   walks on water *WP 110; AM 56*

Philemon *WP 23; SD 83*

Pilate tries Jesus *WP 74*

plagues of Egypt
   (*see under* **Moses**)

plumbline *AM 40; AM 142*

poetry *WP 23*

prayer
   "ask, seek, knock" *WP 50; AM 57*
   friend at midnight *WP 47; SD 105*
   Jesus' teaching on prayer *WP 27; WP 50*
   Pharisee and tax collector *WP 72; SD 52; AM 114*

pride *WP 112; AM 36*

prophecy *WP 26*

proverbs *WP 24; WP 52; SD 80; AM 57*

psalms *AM 51; AM 121*
   antiphonal *SD 118; AM 121*
   creation (Psalm 8) *AM 38*
   Good Shepherd (Psalm 23) *AM 51*
   praise (Psalm 150) *AM 52; AM 121*
   Psalm 18 *AM 52*
   Psalm 69 *AM 52*
   Psalm 97 *SD 118; AM 52*
   Psalm 113 *SD 118*
   Psalm 150 *AM 51; AM 52*
   reading *SD 118*
   thank you *SD 118*
   wise behaviour (Psalm 1) *AM 52*

Quail *WP 77*

INDEX

Rachel *WP* 60

resurrection (*see* Jesus)

resurrection, "I am the ..." *WP* 117

Revelation *WP* 24; *AM* 129

rich man
and Lazarus *SD* 63

Ruth *WP* 11; *WP* 57; *WP* 124; *SD* 63; *SD* 95; *AM* 24; *AM* 54

Samaritan, good *WP* 47; *WP* 55; *WP* 77; *WP* 110; *WP* 119; *SD* 60; *SD* 98; *AM* 88; *AM* 114

Samuel
and Eli *WP* 67; *SD* 109
birth of *SD* 47; *SD* 104
hears God *WP* 59; *AM* 80
life of *WP* 63

Samson *SD* 69; *SD* 97

Saul *WP* 129
becomes king *SD* 107
(*and see* **David**)

selfishness *WP* 112

sermon on the mount *SD* 99; *AM* 51

servant, unforgiving *WP* 59; *SD* 38; *SD* 69

sheep, lost *WP* 47; *WP* 59; *SD* 64; *AM* 49; *AM* 123

sheep and goats *WP* 47; *SD* 38; *SD* 47; *SD* 60

shepherd, good *WP* 117; *AM* 35

Solomon
and Queen of Sheba *AM* 83
wisdom of *SD* 66

son, prodigal *WP* 39; *WP* 47; *WP* 55; *SD* 94; *AM* 59

sons, two *WP* 31

sower *WP* 36; *WP* 47; *WP* 72; *SD* 60; *SD* 66; *SD* 107

spies and Rahab *SD* 110

spies, return of *SD* 99

storm, stilling of *WP* 65; *WP* 119; *AM* 64

Supper, Last *WP* 67
(*and see* **Jesus, death of**)

talents *WP* 47; *WP* 69

teachings of Jesus

Caesar's tax *SD* 117
"Come to me" *SD* 102
forgiveness *WP* 10
giving *WP* 52; *WP* 60
God's care *WP* 96
Holy Spirit *WP* 13
"Let your light shine" *SD* 109
sermon on the mount *SD* 99; *AM* 51
worry *WP* 112; *AM* 36; *AM* 51
(*and see* **"I am" sayings, Jesus as a teacher, parables, prayer**)

Temple, Jesus lost in *WP* 61; *WP* 74; *SD* 44; *SD* 110

temptation of Jesus *AM* 41

things God hates *AM* 57

tongue, control of *SD* 118

transfiguration *WP* 42; *WP* 110; *AM* 40

treasure *WP* 47

truth *WP* 52

vine, "I am the true ..." *WP* 117

water, walking on *AM* 45

way, truth and life, "I am the ..." *WP* 117

wealth *WP* 112; *AM* 36

wedding at Cana *WP* 34; *SD* 39; *SD* 46

weeds *AM* 60

widow of Nain's son *AM* 83; *AM* 110

widow's offering *WP* 60

wisdom *WP* 24
of Solomon *SD* 66

woman bent double *WP* 34; *WP* 61

woman of Shunem's son *AM* 53

woman washing Jesus' feet *WP* 70

woman with a haemorrhage *WP* 115; *SD* 99

workers in the vineyard *SD* 61; *SD* 69

worry *WP* 112; *AM* 36; *AM* 51

writing on the wall *SD* 83; *SD* 113; *AM* 24; *AM* 42; *AM* 139

Zacchaeus *WP* 10; *WP* 40; *WP* 69; *WP* 101; *SD* 87; *SD* 105; *AM* 31; *AM* 32; *AM* 33; *AM* 140

Belshazzar's Feast *by Rembrandt*

ART

Zacchaeus cannot see Jesus owing to the crowd. Misereor Lenten Veil, Alemayehu Bizuneh

Zacchaeus climbs a tree to see Jesus, who asks him to come down and go to his house. Misereor Lenten Veil, Alemayehu Bizuneh

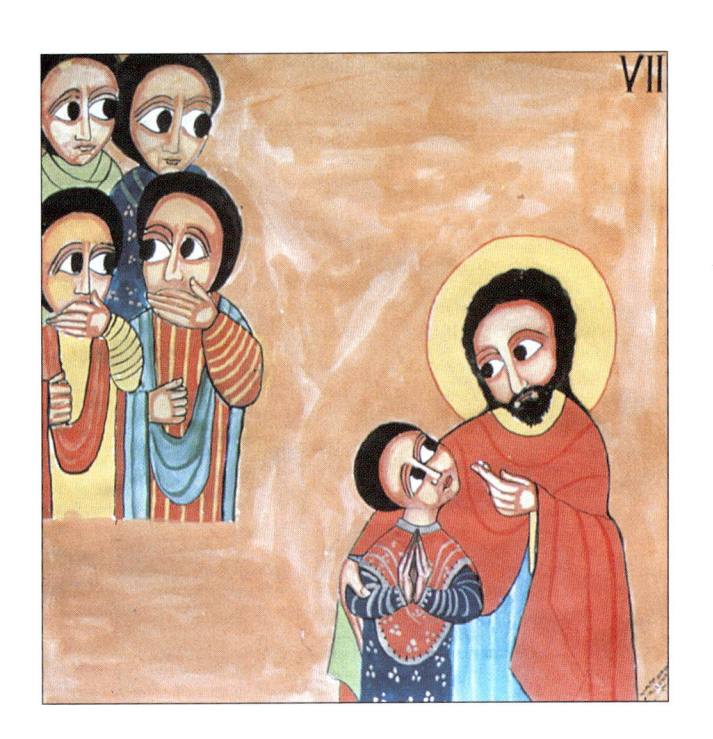

Jesus talks with Zacchaeus. Misereor Lenten Veil, Alemayehu Bizuneh

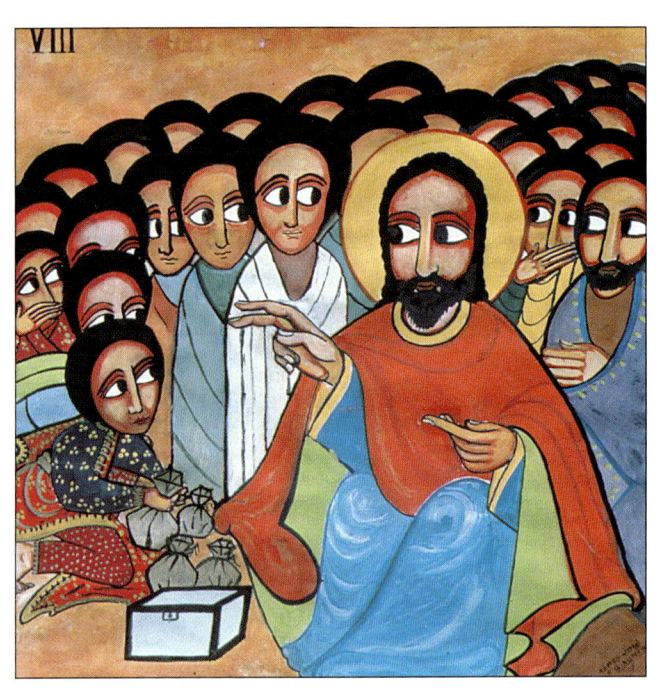

Zacchaeus gives back the money he stole. Misereor Lenten Veil, Alemayehu Bizuneh

The annunciation *by Dante Gabriel Rosetti*

The plumbline and the city from Coventry Cathedral